Contents

geog.1

1 | It's your planet!

geog.1

pages 4-5

The photo below shows planet Earth. Viewing Earth from space allows you to see the Earth as a whole. It's an amazing sight!

1   Write down three words that best describe what Earth looks like from space.

A variety of appropriate words are possible:
huge, round, colourful, cloudy, awesome

2   Imagine you are flying around Earth in a spaceship. Put these three words into a paragraph that best describes what Earth looks like from space.

The answer should incorporate the three words used in the answer to question 1. For the first three words given as examples an answer might be: Planet Earth is huge. From space you can see that it is round, and the clouds can be clearly seen.

3   Identify the five places, A to E, shown on the satellite photo of the earth below.

A North Sea

B France

C Black Sea

D Atlantic Ocean

E Sahara Desert

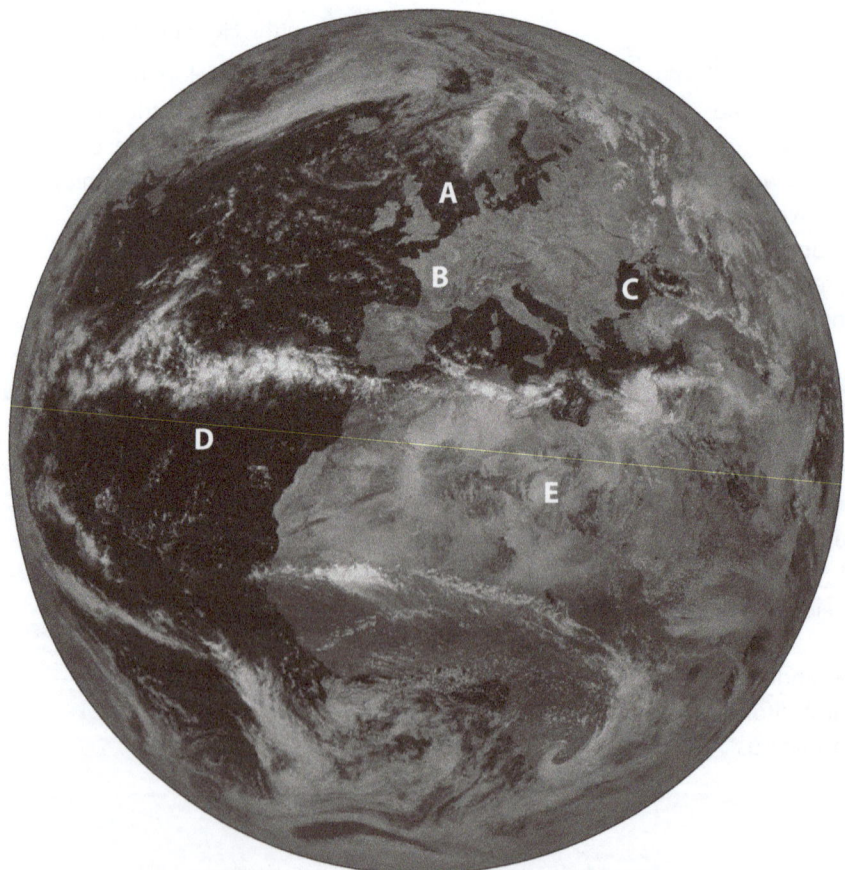

4

This is about how it all started.

geog.1

pages 6-7

1 Read the five sentences below. Circle T or F at the end to say whether they are true or false. Use pages 6-7 in the student book to help you.

a The Big Bang happened about 13 million years ago. T /**F**

b The first star was a hot glowing ball of hydrogen. **T**/ F

c The Sun was formed in a galaxy called the Milky Way. **T**/ F

d The Earth is around 4.5 billion years old. **T**/ F

e The atmosphere around Earth had very little water vapour in it. T /**F**

BANG

2 The paragraph below describes what the Earth was like when it formed. Draw a picture in the space below that shows what you think the Earth looked like. Be as creative as you can!

> The Earth looked very different to today. It would have looked red and orange, not the blue, green and white of today. The surface would have been covered with hot molten rock, the size of many oceans. There was no life, and no water. The atmosphere contained no oxygen, but a mix of deadly poisons.

Red and orange colours should dominate a suitably responsive drawing. Students may choose to show the planet from space with a waterless molten surface and an envelope of toxic clouds, or a close-up on the surface with the molten rocks bubbling and lowering clouds above.

geog.1

pages 8-9

● **From simple cells to humans – this is about the story of evolution.**

1 Look at these statements. They are all about how fossils are formed but are jumbled up. Write a number from 1-6 in the box to put them in the correct order.

Reptile dies	2
Ocean floor is pushed upwards, becoming land	5
Reptile living in ocean	1
Reptile body falls to ocean floor	3
Fossil found by human	6
Reptile buried under mud and sand	4

2 Imagine you are Freddie, a reptile living near the bottom of the ocean waiting to become a fossil. Draw a series of pictures in the spaces below to show how Freddie Fossil was formed and eventually found by a human.

The six drawings should follow the order of the tick boxes above. They should be simple and clear.

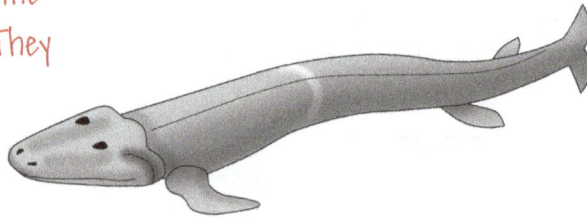

Tip: Remember to put your drawings in the correct order. !

Here you will learn more about the Jurassic period.

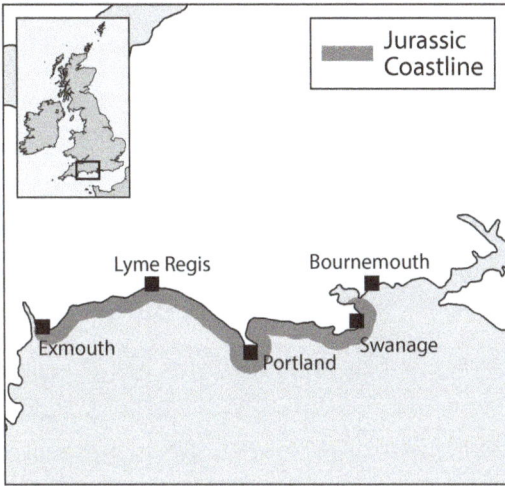

Jurassic Coastline

Lyme Regis

Bournemouth

Exmouth

Portland

Swanage

The map shows the 95 mile long Jurassic Coast of Dorset and East Devon. It is one of the most spectacular coastlines in England, and is so important that it is now a World Heritage site – just like the Great Wall of China! It has classic cliffs, adorable arches and spectacular sea stacks. This part of the coast is the only place on Earth where we can study 185 million years of geological time. It is the finest record of the Triassic, Jurassic and Cretaceous periods in the world.

The topic will be dealt with in geog.2, but students can research in the library or online. Answers should be specific to the Jurassic Coast.

1 Become a detective and do some research about the Jurassic coast. Find out some amazing facts about its arches, its cliffs and the fossils you can find. Write your answers by the side of the arch, cliff and fossil shown below.

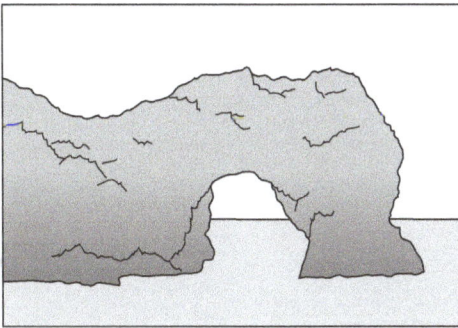

Students may refer to well-known features, such as Durdle Door.

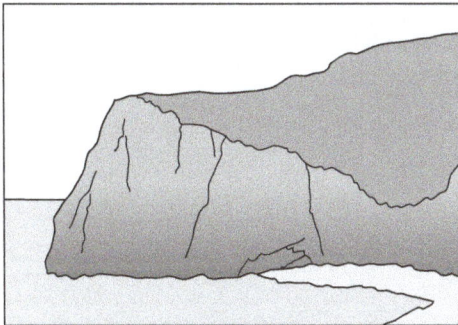

Students may refer to the fossil-bearing cliffs between Bridport and Lyme Regis. They may mention Mary Anning and the discovery of the first ichthyosaurus.

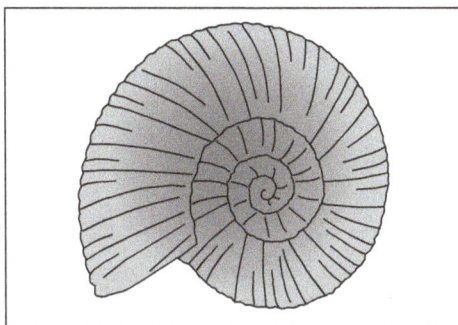

Huge ammonites like this can be seen on the beaches of the Jurassic Coast.

geog.1

pages 12-13

● **This is about humans appearing on Earth.**

1 Early human movement can be called the Journey of Man. Fill in the gaps in these paragraphs. Choose words from the box.

Humans first appeared in East _Africa_. It took us _20 000_ years to reach Britain. However, as we moved 60 000 years ago ice was a problem. Many places were covered in ice _sheets_. The Ice Age was cold so humans left Britain and went to warmer parts of _Europe_. When the ice began to melt, we came back!

Some ocean floor got _drained_ of water which meant that we could walk across areas that used to be sea. Land created like this is often called a land _bridge_. When humans left Africa we had a dark skin, but as we moved away from the _Equator_ the sunlight became weaker and our skin _colour_ changed. Now humans have a range of skin colours across the world!

Equator	drained	Europe	bridge
Africa	colour	20 000	sheets

2 Early man did not have many possessions when making these journeys. Think about possessions or items that might have helped him, what would he have needed?

Label the drawing with your ideas, giving reasons.   Examples are:

Item: Animal skins

Reason: To keep warm

Item: Fire

Reason: For keeping warm and cooking food

Item: Stone tools

Reason: For skinning hides, chopping up meat, and using as spearheads

Item: Containers (made from skin, hollowed wood or pottery

Reason: To hold water, nuts, berries and eggs

This is about where you would like to live.

geog.1
pages 14-15

1 Everybody can think of things that would make a place great to live in. These are often called the *features* of a place. In the box below circle five features that would be important in your ideal place.

Answers will vary.

countryside

leisure centre

railway

shops

park

bus station

roads

industry

cinema

houses

2 In the space below make a sketch of your ideal place to live using the five features that you have chosen.

3 Why have you planned your place like you have? What reasons can you think of to explain? Give as many as you can.

Answers should refer to each of the five features, linking both the sketch and the justification for the features given.

● **This is about where you live – planet Earth!**

1 The earth spins as it travels non-stop around the sun. Why do you not fall off?

I/we do not fall off the earth as it spins

because we are held to it by gravity.

2 Planet Earth is full of life. Fill in the gaps in the following passage using words from the box below.

Elephants are the __*largest*__ land animals on earth. There are only around 600 000

of them left: they are an __*endangered*__ species. New forms of __*life*__ are being

found all of the time. This new life is found on the land and also in the __*oceans*__.

oceans	endangered	largest	life	animal

Did you know, for every one of me, there are 11 166 of you humans out there!

3 Choose one fact about planet Earth. Draw a diagram in the box below to show your chosen fact.

The diagram could be drawn from a photo or drawing in section 1.6, such as the jellyfish or elephant, or it could be based on information in the text such as the earth travelling round the sun at 108 000 km an hour or spinning at 1400 km an hour at the UK.

geog.1

pages 18-19

This is about how natural forces and humans change our planet.

Natural is shown in **bold**.

Hot rocks can change what the landscape looks like.

Factories use valuable resources and sometimes cause pollution.

Water in the river scrapes and shapes the land as it flows.

Villages, towns and cities use a lot of land.

1   a   Each of the photos shows how planet Earth is changing. Under each photo write a caption saying why. Choose from the captions given below.

> Water in the river scrapes and shapes the land as it flows
>
> Villages, towns and cities use a lot of land
>
> Hot rock can change what the landscape looks like
>
> Factories use valuable resources and sometimes cause pollution

b   When you have written your captions, underline the natural reasons in one colour, and the human causes in another.

2   Humans are destroying the Earth. Do you agree?

Students should mention that natural forces are always changing the earth and that some of them can be very destructive. But they are not destroying the earth. Humans are responsible for other problems, as described in the text. Whether these will actually destroy the planet is debatable. Some students might point out that we are more likely to destroy ourselves first!

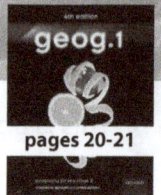

This is about how being nosy could make you a good geographer!

geog.1

pages 20-21

1 Geography can be divided into three different strands, *physical*, *human* and *environmental*. Explain what each one means in your own words.

Students may go to the text in the student book for their definitions or they may choose a dictionary definition.

2 a Now write down any topics you can think of that are part of geography (try to think of at least eight).

Physical examples could include: earthquakes, weather, floods, water, planet earth, atmosphere, fossil fuel, weathering, Big Bang

Human examples could include: work, poverty, crime, agriculture, sport, other countries

Environmental examples could include: pollution, global warming, conservation, waste management, species extinction

b Circle any topics that are *physical* geography in one colour, *human* geography in another, and *environmental* geography in a third.

c Do any of your topics include all three strands? Circle them in a fourth colour.

3 a Have a look at this photo. Underneath, brainstorm questions you could ask about it (can you think of six?).

Suggested questions:

What is she doing?

Is she rich or poor?

What country does she come from?

Does she look as though she is enjoying the work?

Can you think of any good things to say about her job?

What do you think is bad about her job?

b Are you able to answer any of your questions? How would you find answers to the others?

As long as the students have correctly identified the woman as a tea picker, then they can find information on the internet.

Answers will vary for questions 1, 2 and 4.

**Stick a map, or part of a map, in this box.
It can be any sort of map – just as long as it's a map.
Then answer the questions below.**

1 What does your map show?

_____

2 What's the best thing, or most interesting thing, about your map?

_____

3 How would you define a map? Finish this sentence:

A map is _a picture of the earth's surface or part of it on a flat piece of paper._

_____

4 Write down when and how, or why, you last used a map.

_____

_____

This is about how we are connected to people and places all over the world –
and how this can be shown using maps.

geog.1

pages 24-25

Like Walter, you are connected to hundreds of places. Some of them are in Europe.

a Think of five countries in Europe that you have a connection with. List these in the first column of the table.

b In the second column, add the reason for your connection.

c In the table, shade each country a different colour.

d Now shade in the countries on the map that you are connected to. Shade them so that they match your table.

Answers will vary.

Map of Europe with scale 0 300 600 900 km, showing countries labelled: ICELAND, SWEDEN, NORWAY, FINLAND, ESTONIA, RUSSIA, LATVIA, LITHUANIA, DENMARK, IRELAND, NETHERLANDS, BELARUS, UNITED KINGDOM, POLAND, UKRAINE, BELGIUM, GERMANY, CZECH REPUBLIC, SLOVAKIA, SWITZERLAND, MOLDOVA, AUSTRIA, HUNGARY, FRANCE, ROMANIA, PORTUGAL, CROATIA, SLOVENIA, BOSNIA-HERZEGOVINA, SERBIA, BULGARIA, ITALY, KOSOVO, MONTENEGRO, TURKEY, SPAIN, MACEDONIA, ALBANIA, GREECE, MOROCCO, ALGERIA, TUNISIA. Compass with N pointing up.

Country	Connection

A plan of Walter's room

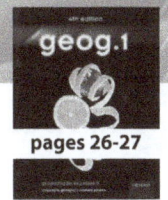

This is about what plans are, and what the scale of the plan tells you.

1   A drawing of something seen from above is called a **plan**.

Match the drawing of a chair with the correct plan (tick the correct one).

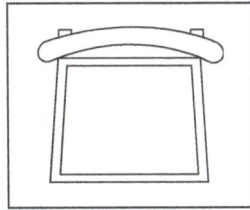

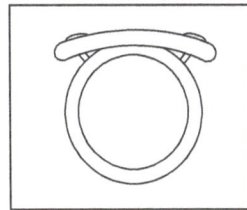

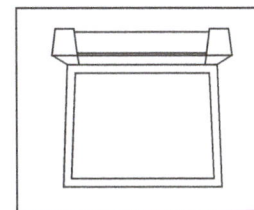

2   Now look at this plan of a bedroom. 1 cm on the plan represents 40 cm in the room. That is the **scale** of the plan.

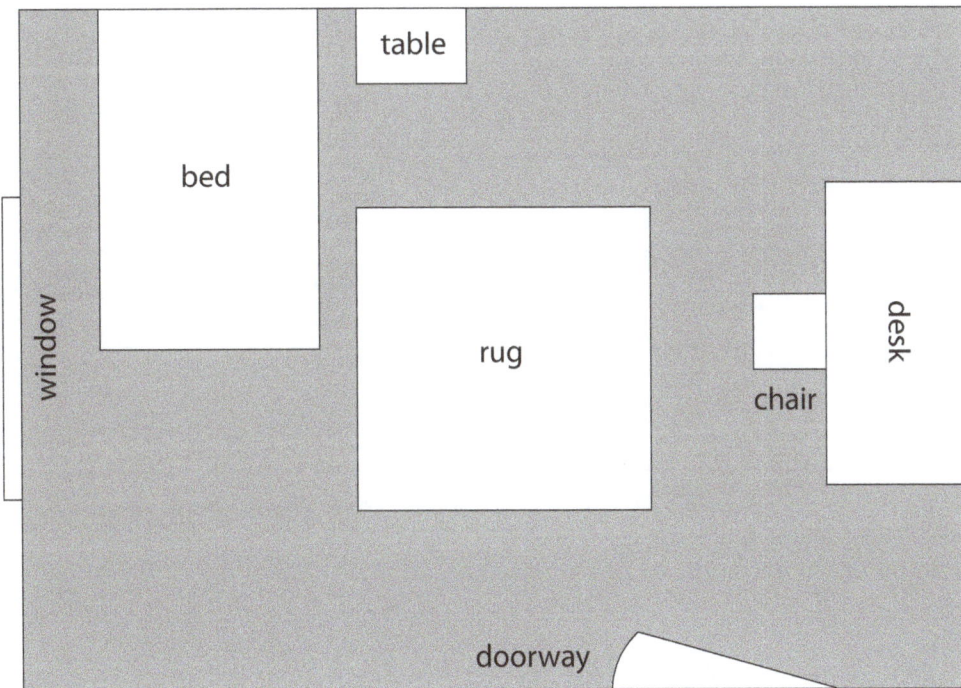

table

bed

window

rug

chair

desk

doorway

0   40   80   120   160 cm

a   On the plan, the window is this wide: ___4 cm___

So, in real life the window is __160__ cm wide. (Fill in the gap.)

b   Now measure the length of the bed and fill in the gaps below.

On the plan, the bed is __4.5__ cm long.

This means it is __180__ cm long in real life.

c   Something in the room is 60 cm wide in real life. What is it? __The table__

d   What in the room is 160 cm x 80 cm in real life? __The desk__

This is about your very own, personal mental maps.

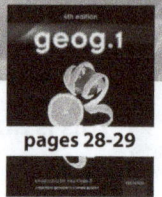

1 **a** Think about a place you know well – it may be your local area or a park for example. In the space below draw a mental map of that area.

> Students may use the map on page 28 of the student book as the basis for their drawing. Credit should be given for imaginative labelling and inventive symbols for showing feelings.

b Add labels to show your feelings about the various parts of your map. Some of your feelings may be happiness, excitement, fear or sadness, but you may be able to think of others as well.

Think of a symbol for each of your feelings and draw the symbol in the correct place on your map.

c Show your map to a partner. Write down the thing that they like best about your map.

_____

_____

_____

_____

This is about how maps are built up.

geog.1

pages 30-31

This photo shows a railway bridge over the River Tamar in Devon.
Your task is to draw a sketch map of the same place.
Don't forget a key!

Students should use section 2.4 for ideas about the key and the sketch map. Labels should be allowed, although they have not been asked for in the rubric.

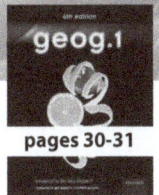

The sketch map and key should show clearly the river, the bridge, the houses, the fields, the trees or woodland and the road that follows the bend of the river.

Key

This is about finding places on a map, using grid references.

1 Fill in the gaps in this sentence, choosing from the words in the box.

A good map has five things: a ___title___, a frame around it, an arrow

to show ___north___, a ___key___ and a ___scale___.

title	note
north	scale
east	lock
key	river

2 Look at this map.

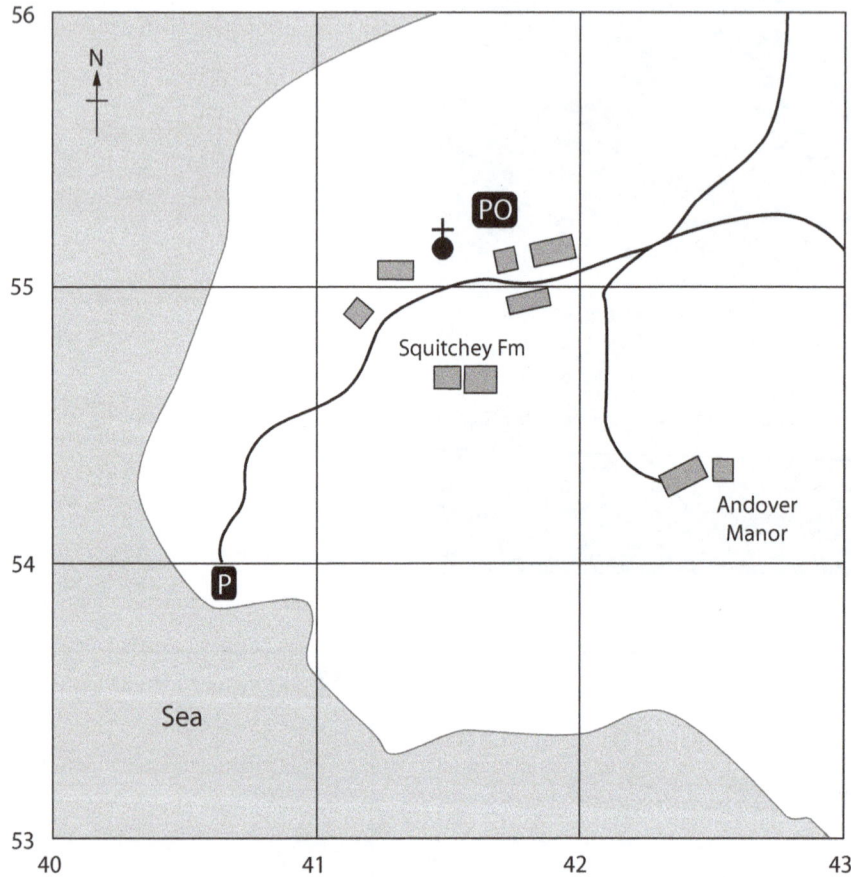

Give a four-figure grid reference for:

a Squitchey Farm ___4154___   **b** Andover manor ___4254___   **c** the church ___4155___

3 What is at this grid reference on the map?

a 407539 ___Parking___   **b** 414552 ___The church___   **c** 416553 ___The post office___

4 Now add two more things to the map. Name them,
and give their six-figure grid reference.

a _____ is at _____

b _____ is at _____

Students can use their imagination here. Two possibilities could be a lighthouse or a school (or an airfield).

This is about how to find the distance between two places on a map.

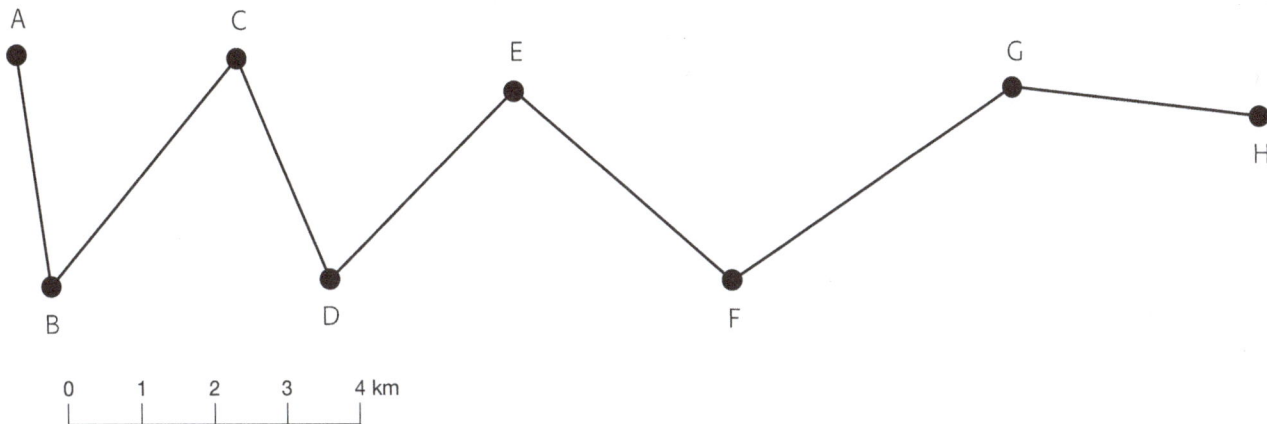

A   C   E   G

B   D   F

0   1   2   3   4 km

1 How far is it as the crow flies:

  a from A to C? _3 kilometres_   **b** from A to H? _17 kilometres_

2 How far is it by road:

  a from A to C? _7 kilometres_   **b** from A to H? _25.5 kilometres_

3 Have a look at the map on page 21.

  a How far is it as the crow flies from Hella Point (in square 3721) to Pordenack

     Point (square 3424)? _7.5 kilometres_

  b How far is it by road between St Buryan (4125) and Trethewey (3823)?

     7.5 kilometres

4 a Follow these instructions.

     Drive east from Land's End for just over a kilometre. Take a right turning and follow the
     road for 1.8 km. Turn left and follow the short track to the end.

     Where do you end up? _Skewjack Farm_

  b Now give instructions (as in **a**) to someone who wants to travel from Treen (3922)
     to Trebehor (3724).

     _Drive west by north west for 4 km through Trethewey. At
     the crossroads turn right and drive 1 km. Then turn right
     and after 500 m you will reach Trebehor._

Which direction?

geog.1

pages 36-37

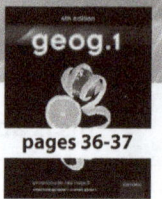

● This is about how to give and follow directions, using N, S, E and W.

1 Draw an arrow going in these directions (**a** has been done for you).

a to the south **b** to the north east **c** to the west **d** to the south west

e to the north west **f** to the east **g** to the north **h** to the south east

2 Look at this grid. Now follow the instructions on the right.

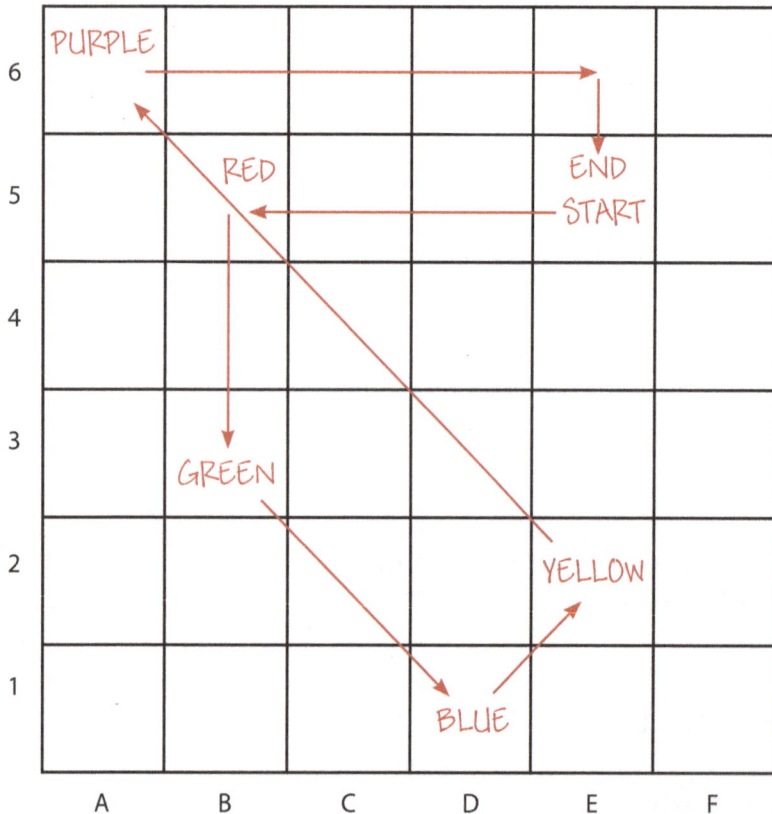

	A	B	C	D	E	F
6	PURPLE					
5		RED			END START	
4						
3		GREEN				
2				YELLOW		
1			BLUE			

● Start in square E5.

● Go three squares W. Colour this square *red*.

● Go two squares S. Colour this square *green*.

● Go two squares SE. Colour this square *blue*.

● Go one square NE. Colour this square *yellow*.

● Go four squares NW. Colour this square *purple*.

● Go four squares E and one square S.
What square do you end up in?

   E5, where I started

3 Name the direction the arrow is coming **from**.

a →   **b** ↓   **c** ↑   **d** ↗

from the _West_   from the _North_   from the _South_   from the _South west_

This is about what OS maps are, and what they show, and how to use them.

This OS map shows part of the Land's End peninsula in Cornwall.

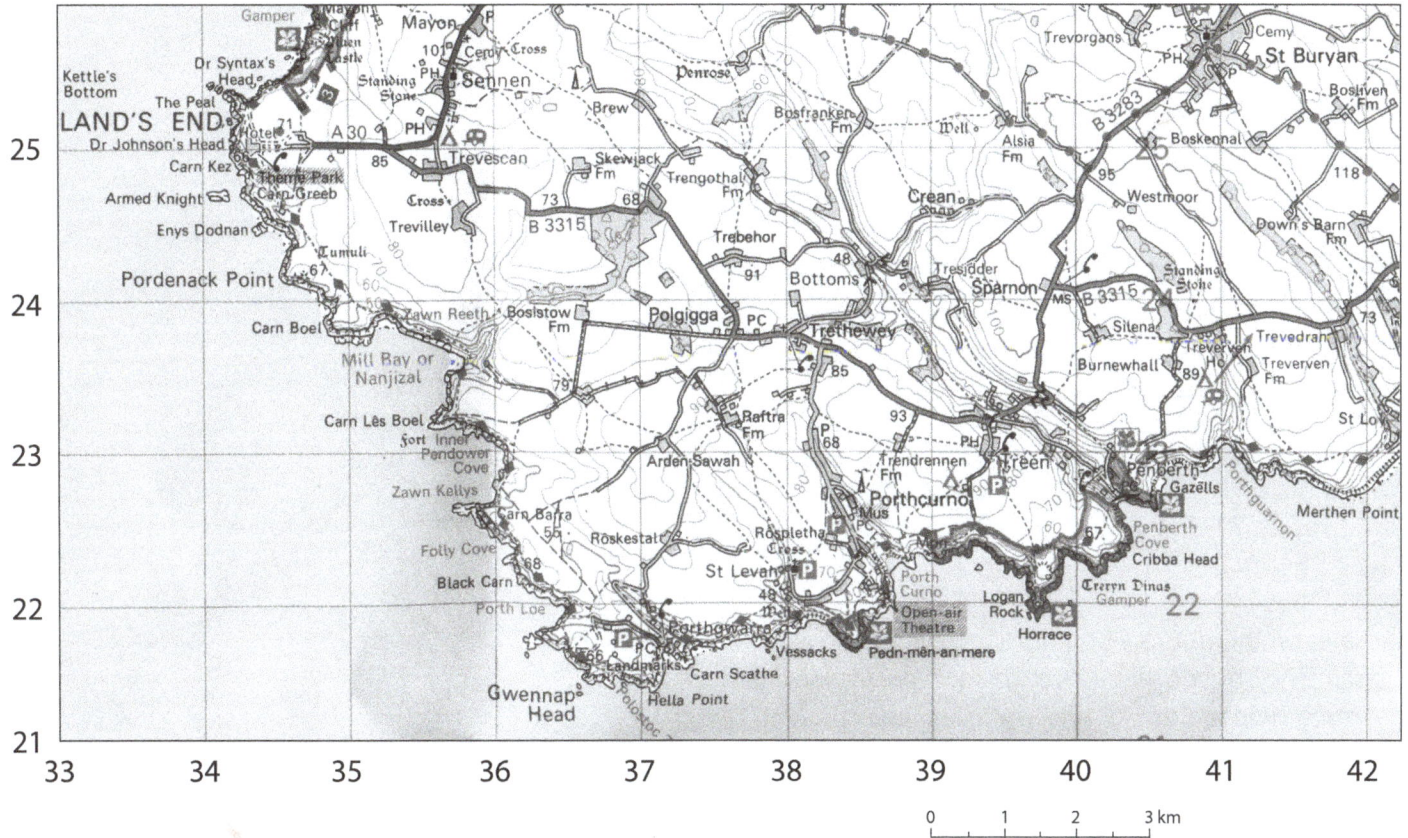

1 What is at this grid reference?

a 387219 _Open air theatre_

c 366249 _Skewjack Farm_

b 385253 (Hint: Fm means farm) _Bosfranken Farm_

d 345242 _Pordenack Point_

2 Find one of these on the map and give a six-figure grid reference for it.

a a car park _381222_

c a public phone _343250_

b a church _409258_

d a camp site _357251_

3 What clues are there on the map that the Land's End peninsula gets lots of visitors? Give as many as you can.

Hotel, Theme park, National Trust land
Public footpath, National Cycle Trail

This is about how height is shown on an OS map.

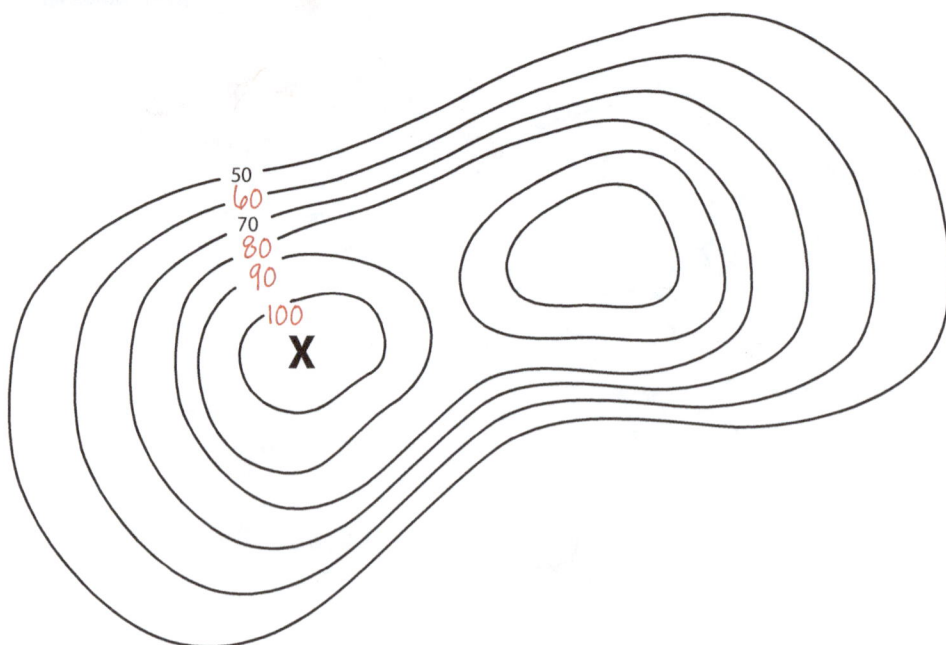

50
60
70
80
90
100
X

1   The lines on this map are contour lines. Everything along a contour line is the same height above sea level. The number on the line shows the height in metres. These contour lines are at 10 m intervals.

a   Write in the four missing labels.

b   Above what height is the land at X? _100 metres_

c   Colour in all the land above 80 metres.

d   Write a label to show where the slope is steep.   It's the slope to the south east of X

e   Now write a label to show where the slope is gentle.   The eastern slope

2   Now look at the OS map on page 21. About how high above sea level is:

a   Trevilley (358246)? _80 metres_

b   Raftra Farm (376233)? _90 metres_

3 a   Complete this sentence:

Another way that OS maps show how high a place is is by using _spot heights:_ _the small black numbers_. These give the exact height at a spot, in metres above sea level.

b   Can you find an example of this on the OS map on page 21? Give a four-figure grid reference.   Example below.
3823 = 68 metres

Where on Earth are you?

geog.1

pages 42-43

This is about the special grid lines we use to say where places are on Earth.

1 Cross out the wrong word in these sentences.

a The lines that circle the Earth from top to bottom are lines of longitude / ~~latitude.~~

b The lines that circle the Earth from side to side are lines of ~~longitude~~ / latitude.

c The 0° line of latitude is called the Equator / ~~Arctic Circle.~~

d The 0° line of longitude is called the ~~Equator~~ / Prime Meridian.

2 Write these statements as coordinates:

a 33° north of the Equator, 20° east of the Prime Meridian.   33°N 20'E

b 44° south of the Equator, 40° west of the Prime Meridian.   44°S 40'W

3 Look at the map.

a Finish labelling the lines of latitude.

b Label the five main lines of latitude: the Equator, the Tropic of Cancer, the Tropic of Capricorn, the Arctic Circle, and the Antarctic Circle.

c Now finish labelling the lines of longitude.

d Label the Prime Meridian.

e Shade the area between the Tropic of Cancer and the Tropic of Capricorn in a 'warm' colour. Label this region 'The tropics'.

f Shade the Arctic and Antarctica in a 'cool' colour. Label these regions.

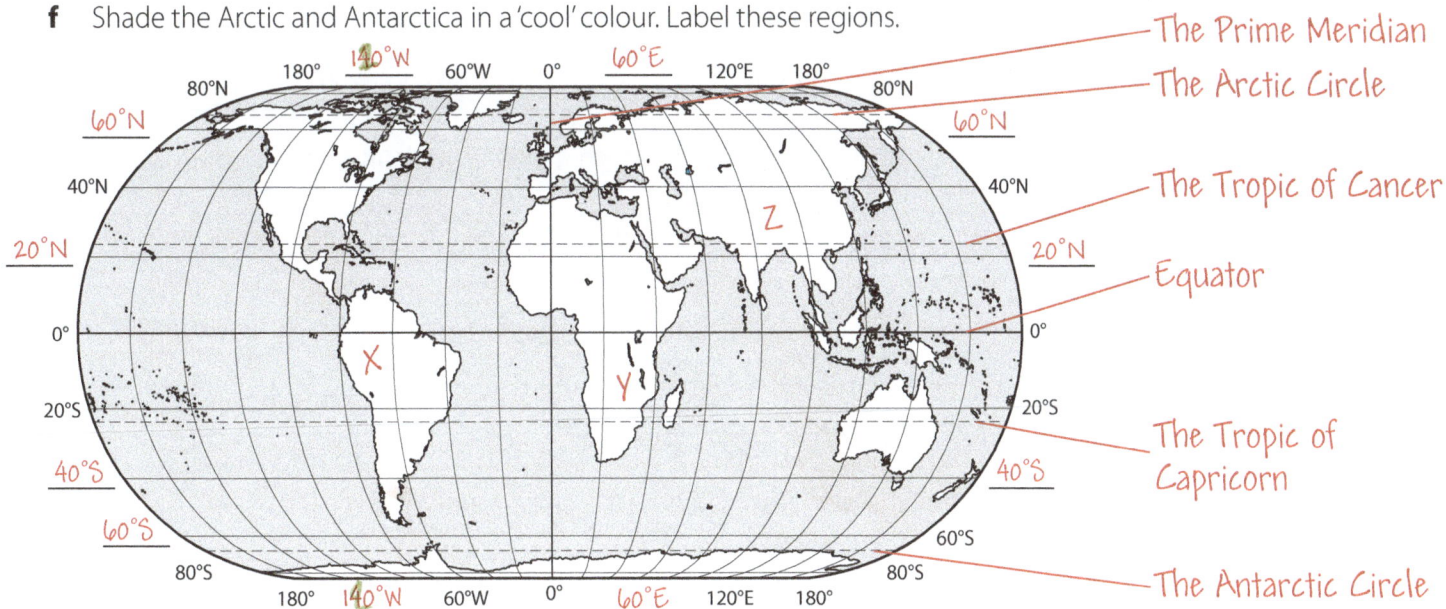

4 Mark three dots on the map, each one in a different continent.
Label them X, Y, and Z. Write the coordinates of your places here: Answers will vary. For example:

X 4°S 70'W   Y 8°S 30'E   Z 36°N 100'E

What about the UK?

1 Here are traditional flowers or plants associated with the countries of the UK. Can you say which part of the UK they stand for?

Scotland

Northern Ireland

England

Wales

2 What is your image of the UK? Write down the words or phrases that come to mind when you think of the UK under the headings below.

Sport Cycling, Sailing, Swimming, Golf, Football, Rugby, Cricket, Athletics, Rowing

Music Rock (blues, punk), Folk (English, Celtic), Bhangra, Brit pop, Classical (Early, Baroque, choral)

Achievements/Inventions Far too numerous to list! But Wikipedia has a good entry which lists 'British inventions' under categories. Apart from well-known historical and recent inventions (e.g. Steam and Jet engines, World Wide Web) there are surprisingly many modern inventions (e.g. DNA profiling).

Famous people Students will have their own idea of what constitutes fame! But worth pointing out how famous around the world many of our scientists and inventors have been (not just footballers and pop stars!) The royal family is, of course, famous too.

Food Fish and chips, bangers and mash, chicken tikka masala, pizza, pork pies, sweet and sour chicken, fast food, plus many regional variations.

This is about the forces that shaped the British Isles – and about Britain's main physical features.

1 This paragraph explains how our island home became an island.
Choose words from the box to fill in the gaps.

Once upon a time, the British Isles lay at the _equator_, as part of a giant _continent_. When this broke up, they drifted _north_ as part of Europe. As they drifted, over millions of years, they went through many _changes_. They became desert. They were frozen in _ice_. They were drowned by the _sea_. They had earthquakes and eruptions. They got pushed and squeezed until _mountains_ grew. And then they got _cut off_ from the rest of Europe.

ice	cut off	changes	sea
crust	continent	mountains	currents
north	equator		

2 Here are some features of the British Isles, but they're all jumbled up.
Unscramble the words and then use them to label the map below.

vrier sernve   verri nttre
rierv htmaes   alke drictist
eisglhn nanchel   ninespen
rthno aes   rthno estw landshigh
isirh sae

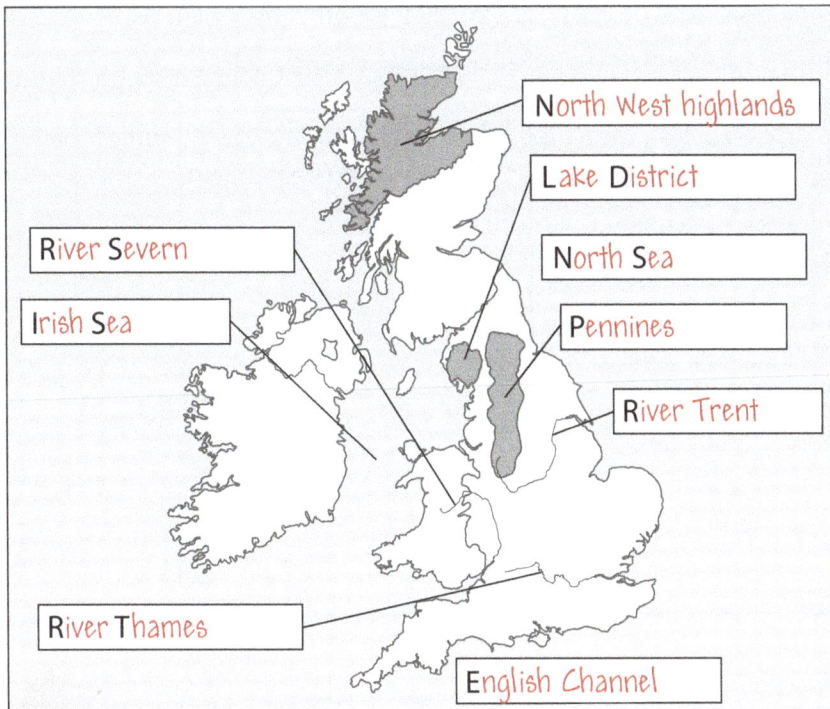

North West highlands
Lake District
River Severn
North Sea
Irish Sea
Pennines
River Trent
River Thames
English Channel

It's a jigsaw!

This is about how we humans have carved up the British Isles.

1 Fill in the gaps using words from the box.

The British Isles is divided up into two countries: the United Kingdom and the
Republic of Ireland.

The _United Kingdom_ in turn is made up of different nations: England,
Scotland, Wales and Northern Ireland.

United Kingdom	Germany	British Isles
Republic of Ireland	Scotland	England

2 Now look at the map and answer these questions.

a A is called
Scotland

b B is called
England

c D is called
Northern Ireland

d A–D together are called
The United Kingdom

e A–E together are called
The British Isles

f Finally, shade in the countries that make up Great Britain.

3 Draw a line on the map to the country or region that you live in and label it.
What is special about your country or region?

Answers will vary. Students may describe their region as their city, their county
or their wider region (e.g. the South West).

What's our weather like?

This is about the difference between weather and climate – and how the climate varies across the UK.

1 Fill in the gaps.

- _Weather_ means the state of the _atmosphere_ . Is it warm? wet? windy?

  It changes from day to day.

- _Climate_ is the _average_ weather in a place.

weather	average	atmosphere	climate

2 **a** Cross out the wrong word in these sentences.
In general:

- It is colder/~~warmer~~ in the north, because it is further from the equator.
- It is also colder/~~warmer~~ on high land. Up a mountain the temperature falls/~~rises~~.
- But in winter, a ~~cold~~/warm ocean current called the North Atlantic Drift ~~cools~~/ warms the west coast. So the east coast is the coldest/~~warmest~~ part in winter.

b The maps below show average temperatures in summer and winter. Colour in the first map in shades of orange. Make the warmest areas darkest, and the coldest areas lightest. _Darkest orange in the south, lightest orange in the north._

c Now colour the second map in blue. This time, make the coldest areas darkest. And don't forget the key! _Darkest blue in the east/north east, lightest blue in the west/south west._

3 Answer these questions in full sentences.

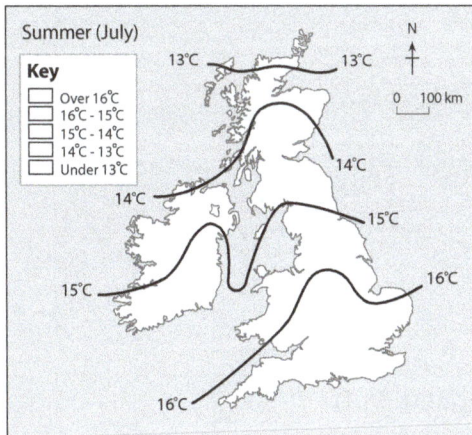

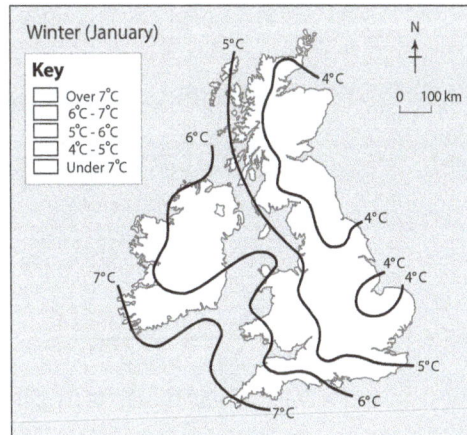

Summer (July)

Key
- Over 16°C
- 16°C - 15°C
- 15°C - 14°C
- 14°C - 13°C
- Under 13°C

N

0   100 km

13°C   13°C
14°C
14°C   15°C
15°C   16°C
16°C

Winter (January)

Key
- Over 7°C
- 6°C - 7°C
- 5°C - 6°C
- 4°C - 5°C
- Under 7°C

N

0   100 km

5°C
4°C
6°C
4°C
7°C   4°C   4°C
5°C
6°C
7°C

a Which parts of the British Isles are wettest?

The western parts of the British Isles are the wettest. Wettest of all are the moors and mountains of the South West, Wales, the North West and the Scottish Highlands.

b Can you explain why?
The prevailing wind is from the south west. The rain falls on the windward side of high ground. The leeward side is in the rain shadow and stays quite dry.

Who are we?

This is about how Britain has been peopled by immigrants.

1   Some of the definitions below are incorrect, but which? Cross out any wrong terms and write the correct word in the second column. One has been done for you.

	Correct term
A An **asylum seeker** is a person who flees to another country for safety, and asks to be allowed to stay there.	
B An **invader** is someone who enters a country to attack it.	
C An ~~emigrant~~ is a person who comes into a country to live.	immigrant
D A **settler** is a person who takes over land to live on, where no one has lived before.	
E A **refugee** is a person who has been forced to flee from danger.	
F An ~~asylum seeker~~ is a person who leaves his or her own country to settle in another country.	emigrant
G A ~~refugee~~ is a person who moves to another part of the country or another country, often just to work for a while.	economic migrant

2   Here are some statements from people who've arrived in the British Isles in the last 2000 years.

It's 48 AD. I am a centurion with the Roman army. Our aim is to expand our empire.

Invader

I came to live here a few years ago, in 2001. I didn't want to leave Kosovo but the war meant it was too dangerous to stay.

Asylum seeker

It's 1956. I've come here from Jamaica in search of a job.

Economic migrant

It's 4000 BC. I've come here from Europe with my tribe. We're looking for a good place to farm.

Settler

Choose what you think is the best term for each person (use terms from question 1).

3   Do you agree with this statement: 'In the British Isles, we are all immigrants'?

The flow chart on page 52 of the student book shows how the British Isles were populated by waves of migration, so the most likely answer is 'Yes'. Students should go on to point out the different kinds of immigrant we have received and (hopefully) how much we have benefitted from them.

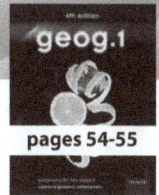

This is about how we humans have shaped the country, through where we chose to live!

pages 54-55

1 Fill in the gaps.

The ___population___ ___density___ of a place is the average number of people per square kilometre.

2 Tick the correct answer.

a The nation with the highest population density is …

England ✓   Wales ☐   Scotland ☐

b Of these areas, the one with the lowest population density is …

Cumbria ✓   Greater Manchester ☐   Devon ☐

c Of these cities, the largest is …

Edinburgh ☐   Birmingham ✓   Glasgow ☐

3 Look at this pie chart for the United Kingdom.

Where the UK population lives

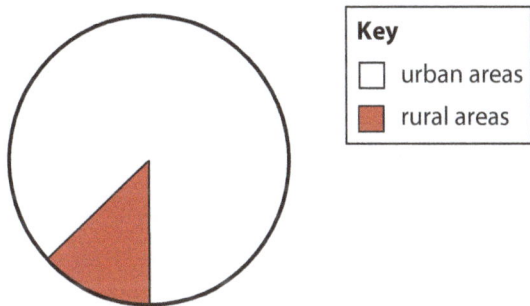

Key
☐ urban areas
▨ rural areas

a Shade in the chart and the key to show where the population of the UK lives.

b Imagine you live on a farm half an hour's drive to the nearest town.
Give three good points and three bad points about living in such a rural area.

Good points
Suggestions are:

Beauty of the countryside; peace and quiet; lots of space;

healthy environment; close to nature

Bad points
Suggestions are:

Long distance to the shops; schools; hospitals etc. Isolation and loneliness;

poor internet and mobile phone coverage/connection; poor public transport

How are we doing?

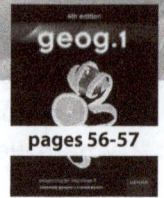

This is about how some parts of Great Britain are better off than others – and some of the reasons why.

geog.1

pages 56-57

House prices, wages and unemployment vary from region to region in the UK.

Region	average house price (£)	average wage (£ per week)	unemployment (%)
A Wales	164 200	453	8.0
B Scotland	185 000	498	7.3
C Northern Ireland	129 700	460	7.3
D North East	149 400	455	10.3
E North West	165 600	470	8.6
F Yorks & Humber	167 300	465	8.8
G East Midlands	177 650	465	7.7
H West Midlands	187 800	470	9.4
I East	257 000	495	5.9
J London	436 550	650	8.6
K South East	304 000	540	6.0
L South West	230 400	467	6.3

* 2013 figures

1 Complete the bar chart below for house prices and wages in 2013. Wales has been done for you.

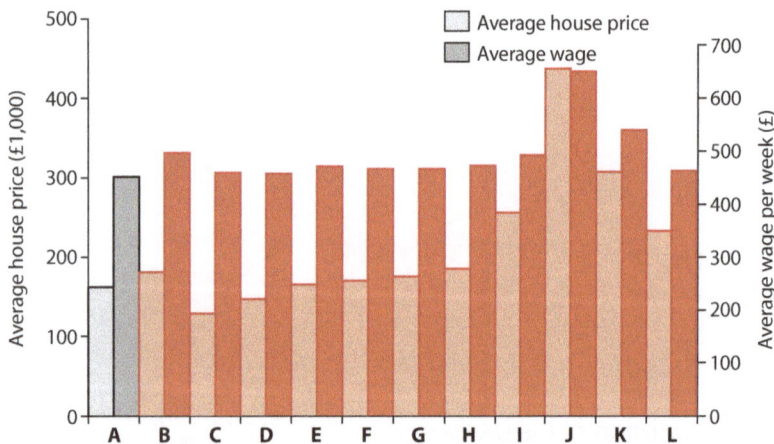

2 What do the differences in house prices tell you about inequality in the UK?

On their own they tell you that people who own property in London and the South East are wealthier than people in other regions. Inequality is implied, but students may mention that large mortgages and greater debt may mean the picture is less clear than appears at first sight.

3 What does the relationship between house prices and wages tell you about inequality in the UK?

The gap between house prices and wages is less in the regions where the house prices are lowest. This should make it easier for someone to afford a house. So, the perceived inequality between London and the rest is not as great as it first appears.

4 With the unemployment figures in mind as well, which region of the UK do you think would be the best to live in for income, employment and affordable housing? Why?

Some students may decide that Northern Ireland, with its relatively low unemployment rate and relatively large gap between house prices and wages, is a good region in which to live.

geog.1

pages 58-59

This is about the London marathon. Can you work out its route from a description?

The London marathon is the most popular marathon in the world. In 2013 there were 35 000 runners.

1 Read this description of the route of a recent London Marathon. Then trace the route of the race on the map below. Write in the words 'Start' and 'Finish'. Write in the missing words in the description and insert the numbers in the correct places on the map.

The race starts in Greenwich Park, south of the river and just to the east of the well-known loop of the Thames at the Isle of Dogs. The runners head east, across the A2 to _Charlton_ park. (1) At the A _4205_ (2) road the race turns north, towards the river and then turns west along _Woolwich_ Church Street (3). They pass Maryon _Park_ (4) and run along the A206, over the A2 again and towards Greenwich once more where they run past the famous ship, the Cutty _Sark_ (5). They then turn north-west, until they get to the old docks at Surrey _Quays_ (6). They then follow the loop of the river past the _Rotherhithe_ Tunnel (7). Heading west along the river past Bermondsey, they cross the Thames at _Tower_ Bridge (8). They now head east again past Wapping, and turn south into the Isle of Dogs, running along the Westferry Road. At the southernmost point of the loop they turn north, running towards the well-known skyscraper of Canary _Wharf_ (9) Near the _Blackwall_ Tunnel (10) they turn west, heading for Limehouse. They then follow the Thames. They are now in the old City of _London_ (11). Still heading west they run past Waterloo Bridge. From here they can see the National Theatre and the Royal Festival Hall on the _South_ _Bank_ (12). At _Westminster_ near the Houses of Parliament, they head away from the river towards St James Park. They run clockwise around the lake and the race ends at the northern end of the park.

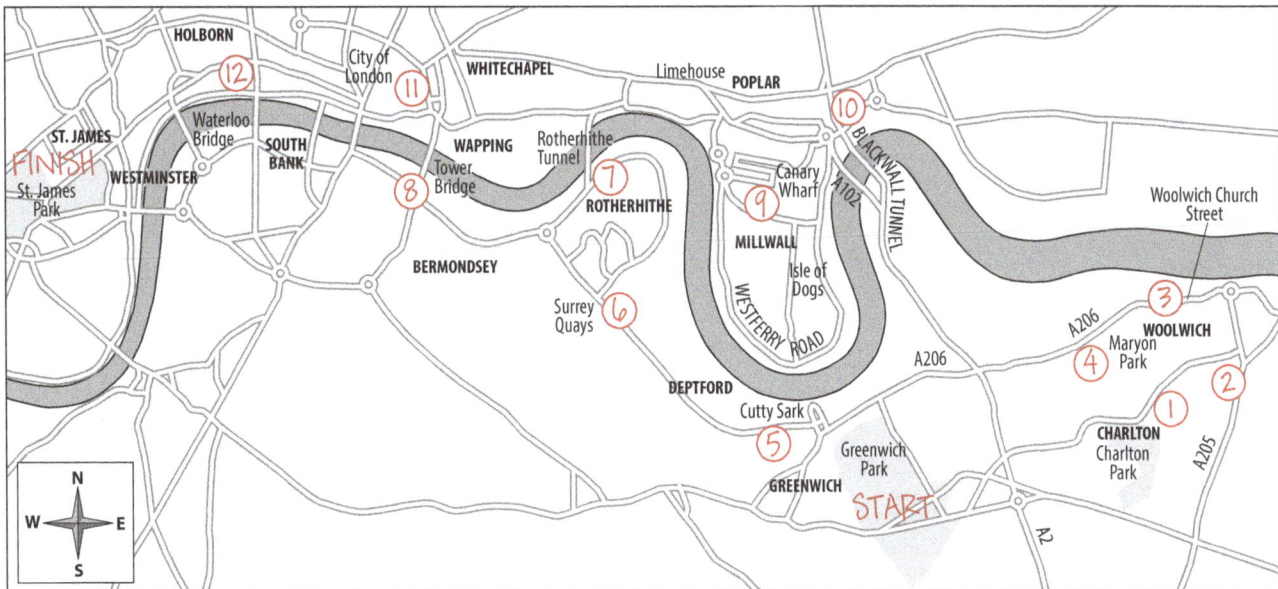

4 Glaciers

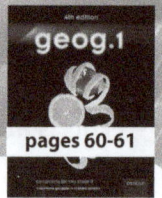

Find the best photo of a glacier you can, and stick it in this space!

1 Write down two things you know about glaciers.

A variety of answers here: rivers of ice; made of frozen fresh water; help to shape the land.

2 Write down two things you'd like to find out about glaciers.

Possible answers are; Where are they found? How long are they? What happens when they retreat?

At the end of this topic, come back and see if you've found out about these things. If you have, draw a ☺ next to your question – if you haven't, draw a ☹!

This is about understanding when the British Isles was in the grip of ice.

Seen any mammoths?

Yep!

1   Write 'True' or 'False' in the box after each of these sentences.

   a   Woolly mammoth once roamed southern Britain.   True

   b   Woolly mammoth were like very large sheep.   False

   c   A few woolly mammoth can still be found in remote parts of Scotland.   False

   d   Woolly mammoth were like hairy elephants.   True

2   Finish this timeline. The good thing is that the 'time' labels are already in place. To finish it, you need to add notes at each time label, saying what was happening at that time.

Today

10 000 years ago — Earth had warmed up again as the Ice Age ended.

12 000 years ago — Humans came back to the British Isles as the ice sheet shrank.

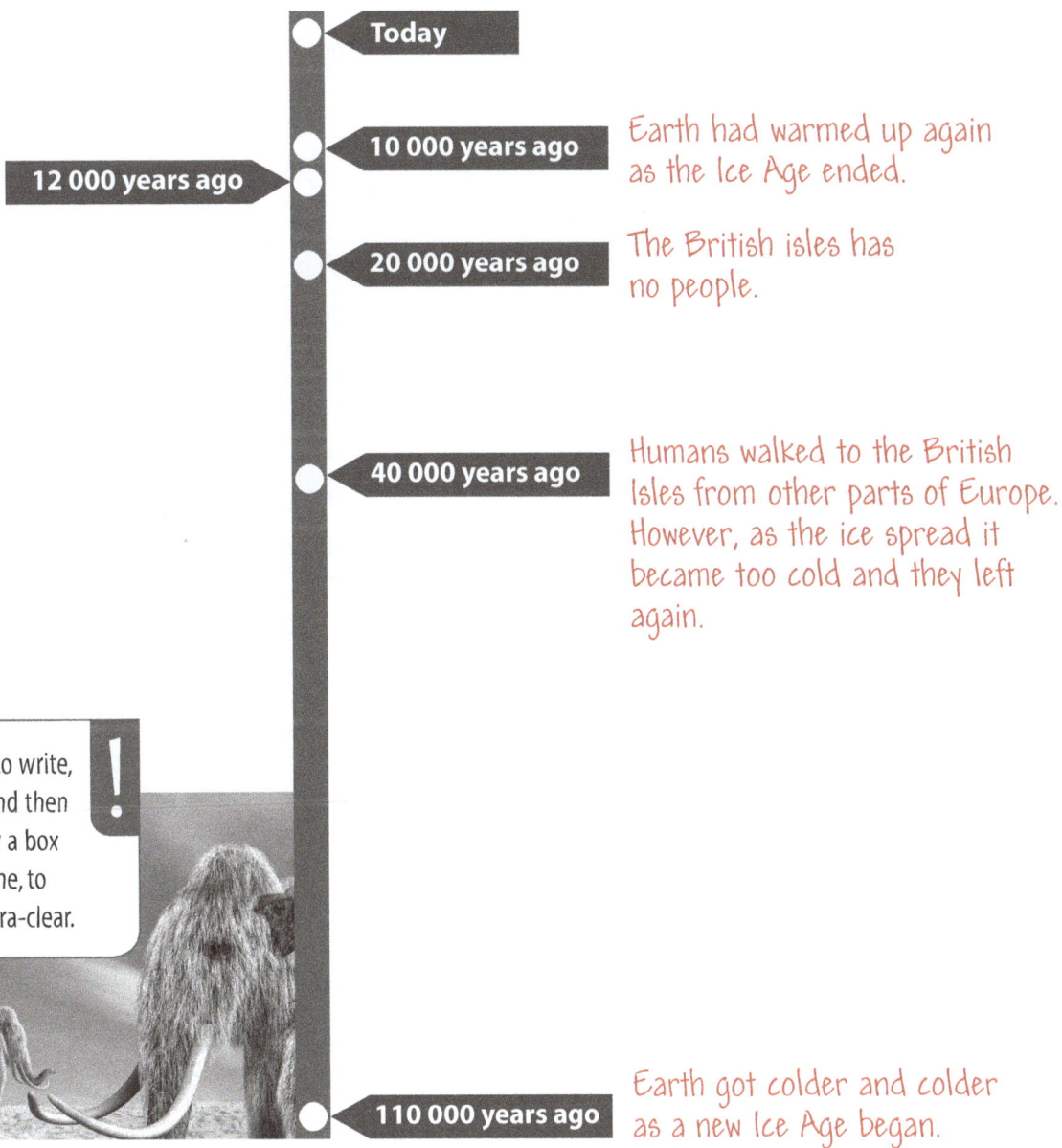

20 000 years ago — The British isles has no people.

40 000 years ago — Humans walked to the British Isles from other parts of Europe. However, as the ice spread it became too cold and they left again.

Tip: Plan what you're going to write, before you start writing – and then write neatly! You could draw a box round your notes at each time, to help make your timeline extra-clear.

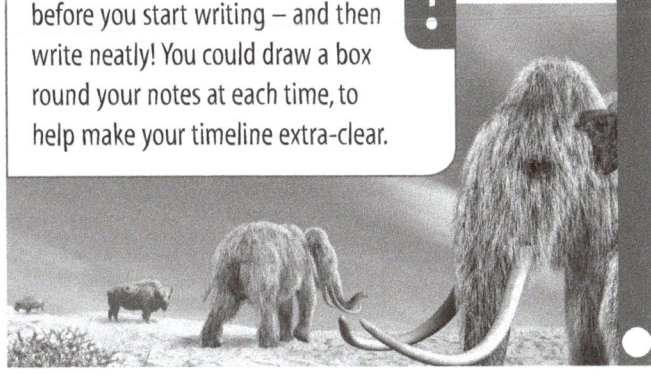

110 000 years ago — Earth got colder and colder as a new Ice Age began.

4.2 Glaciers

This is about the world's glaciers today.

1 Tick the correct answer:

a How much of the Earth's surface do glaciers cover?

about 40% ☐   about 30% ☐   about 20% ☐   about 10% ✓

b During the last ice age, how much of the Earth's surface was covered by glaciers?

about 43% ☐   about 33% ✓   about 25% ☐   about 20% ☐

c Today, how much of the world's ice is in Antarctica and Greenland?

less than 90% ☐   95% ☐   99% ☐   over 99% ✓

d What are large cracks in glaciers are called?

cravats ☐   crevasses ✓   crevices ☐   creases ☐

e How many continents have glaciers?

two ☐   three ☐   five ☐   all seven ✓

2 Do some research to find out about Vatnajokull Glacier in Iceland.

Find a photo of Vatnajokull Glacier and stick it in the big box below, and then write a fact about Vatnajokull in each of the smaller boxes.

A variety of answers is possible. Possibilities include: Europe's largest glacier; surface area of 8,100 square km; the glacier hides some active volcanoes; the ice cap rises to over 2000 m above sea level and is found at 300 m below sea level.

geog.1

pages 66-67

This is your chance to show that you know how glaciers shape the landscape.

1 Draw a spider diagram to show the work that glaciers do and how they do it. The first one has been started for you.

Tip: A good way to do this would be to start with the three jobs glaciers do.

Ice freezes …

Students should construct a spider diagram like that below.

Erosion

Answers should address the three main actions carried out by glaciers: they pick up or erode material, transport it away and then drop or deposit it elsewhere.

Tip: You could colour-code the different parts of your spider diagram – this would help make it even clearer.

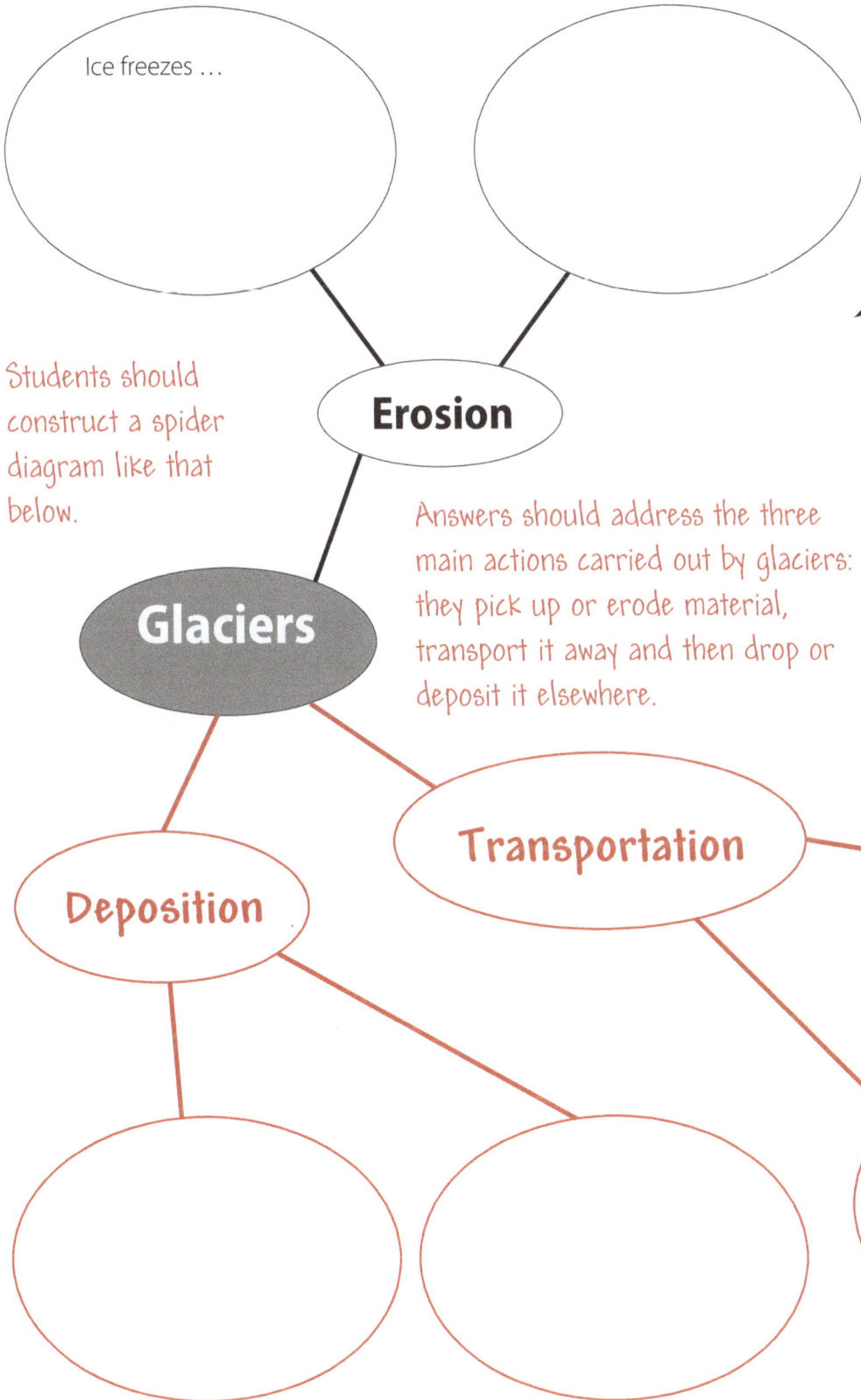

Glaciers

Transportation

Deposition

Glacial landforms created by erosion: part 1

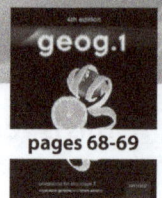

● **This is your chance to learn how glaciers can change the landscape.**

1 The paragraph below describes how a corrie is formed.
Circle the correct word from each pair.

As snow falls, it **compacts** / **constructs** into ice. Through **abrasion** / **corrosion** the hollow gradually becomes **bigger** / **smaller** and the walls steeper. Eventually, with the help of freeze-thaw, the glacier is big enough to flow over the **edge** / **bottom** of the corrie and move down the mountain. When the glacier melts, the corrie often has a **lake** / **river** in it. This is often called a tarn.

2 Imagine you are going on an expedition to explore Bleaberry Tarn in the Lake District, shown in Photo A on page 68 in the student book. Write down five things that you think you would need to take to help make your expedition a success.

A variety of answers is possible. Expect responses related to clothing, footwear, food, maps or GPS devices. For each of the items listed, pupils should give some justification for its inclusion.

Give a reason for each of your answers.

I would need to take...	because...
1	
2	
3	
4	
5	

3 Study the photograph of Bleaberry Tarn again. Imagine you work for the Lake District Tourism Board. You have been asked to write about fifty words to describe what the photograph shows.

Tip: Remember to use as many adjectives (describing words) as you can.

A variety of answers are again possible. A typical descriptive answer might be: Bleaberry Tarn is a corrie lake in the Lake District. It is on high land and overlooks Crummock Water. The land around is not farmed and is just grassland. Footpaths cross the area and lead to the tarn, which shows that it gets visitors walking to it. It is very secluded but also very beautiful.

More ways in which glaciers can change the landscape!

1 Look at photos A and B. Write down three differences between the valleys shown in each photo.

Answers could relate to the shape of the valley, its size or the physical (e.g. vegetation) or human (e.g. footpaths) features.

Tip: Think about the shape of the valleys.

A

B

1 *Photograph A shows a V-shaped valley.*

2 *Photograph B is a U-shaped valley.*

3 *The valley in photograph A has trees along the sides but there are a few in the U-shaped valley.*

2 Look at the map of the Lake District shown below. In your own words describe three facts about the lakes and where they are found. Remember to use the north arrow to help you.

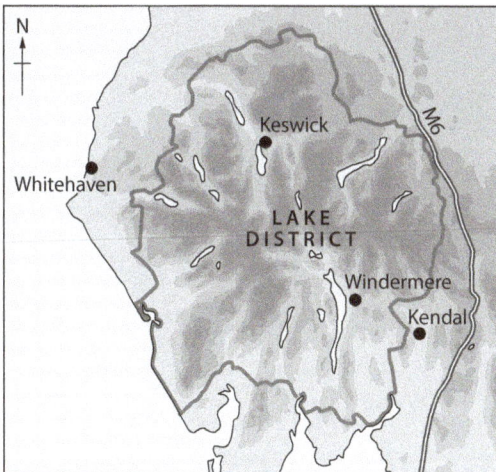

Answers should relate to the map given. A variety of facts that could be given including:
The lakes are in a radial or circular pattern; most of the lakes are long and thin; all of the lakes are found west of the M6 motorway; all lakes are east of the town of Whitehaven.

geog.1

pages 72-73

● **This is where you learn about landforms created when glaciers melt.**

1 Glaciers form many landforms, even when they melt! Complete the fact sheet below that describes and explains the landforms that are created.

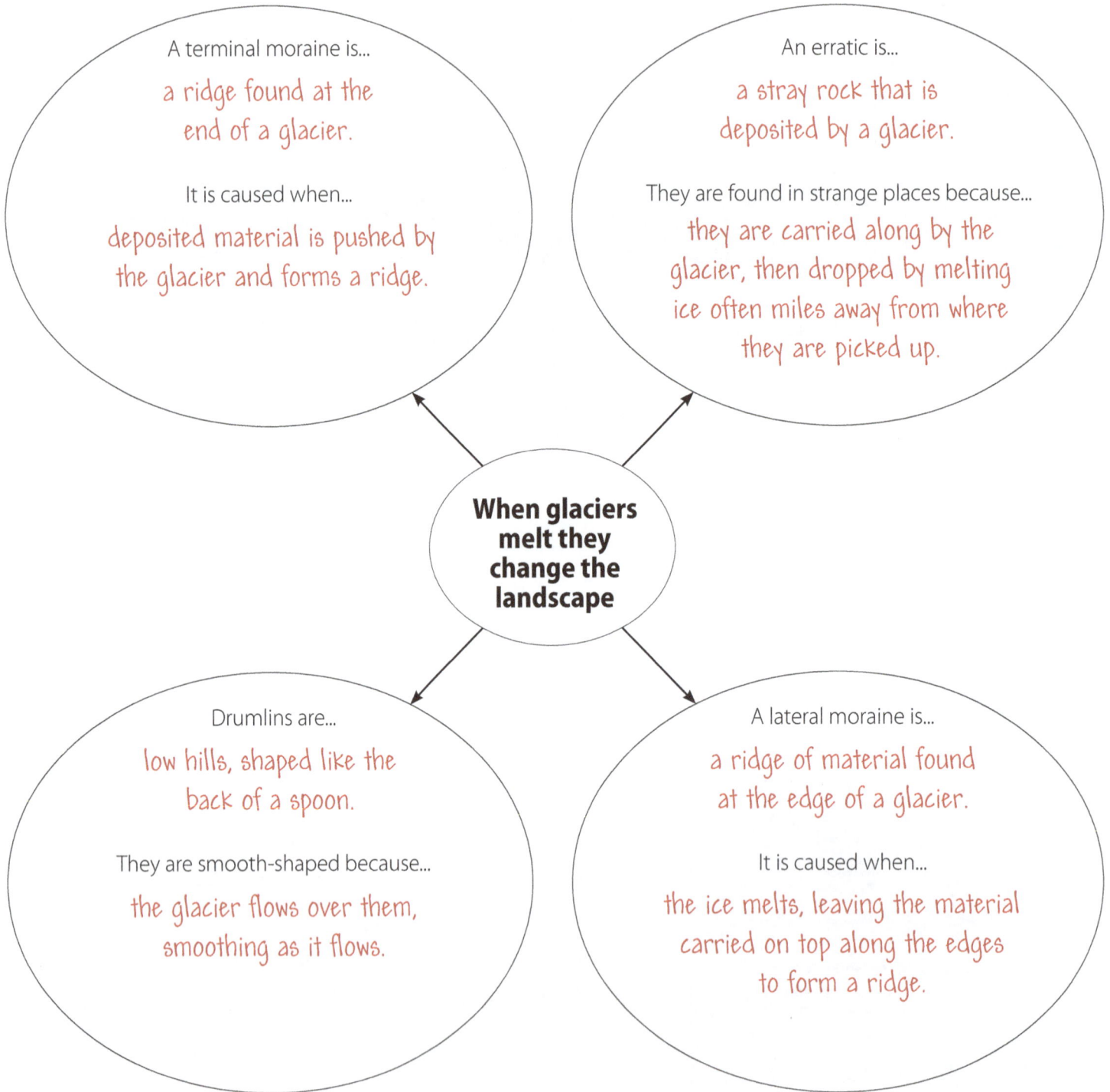

A terminal moraine is...

a ridge found at the end of a glacier.

It is caused when...

deposited material is pushed by the glacier and forms a ridge.

An erratic is...

a stray rock that is deposited by a glacier.

They are found in strange places because...

they are carried along by the glacier, then dropped by melting ice often miles away from where they are picked up.

When glaciers melt they change the landscape

Drumlins are...

low hills, shaped like the back of a spoon.

They are smooth-shaped because...

the glacier flows over them, smoothing as it flows.

A lateral moraine is...

a ridge of material found at the edge of a glacier.

It is caused when...

the ice melts, leaving the material carried on top along the edges to form a ridge.

2 Write and present a two minute talk for your class about one of the landforms created by glaciers – either through glacial erosion or deposition. You should produce one diagram or PowerPoint slide to help you.

A talk should last for two minutes and should use one diagram or slide as a prompt.

This is your chance to become a detective to find glacial landforms on an OS map.

1   Here is the description of a place shown on the map in the student book on page 75. Where is it? Use the clues to help you.

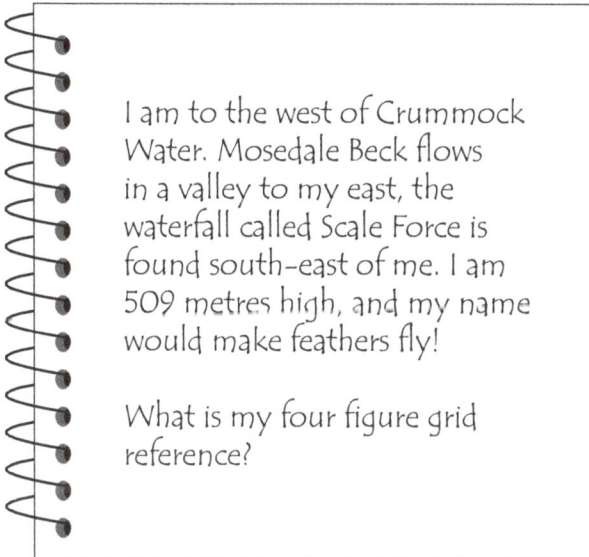

> I am to the west of Crummock Water. Mosedale Beck flows in a valley to my east, the waterfall called Scale Force is found south-east of me. I am 509 metres high, and my name would make feathers fly!
>
> What is my four figure grid reference?

The place is called ___Hen Comb___

The four figure grid reference for it is ___1318___

2   Now write your own clues to describe a place or feature shown on the map. Then test them on a partner. Can they identify it using your clues?

3   Use the clues below to follow a route around the area shown by the map. Write the places that you reach in the blank spaces in the paragraph. Remember to use the clues and the scale to help you!

I start walking from the car park at the Gatesgarth at 6-figure grid reference ___195150___ . I follow the road north-west until I get to the hotel in the village of ___Buttermere___ in grid square 1716. Here, I take the footpath on my left that crosses the valley floor and goes through the forest called ___Burtness___ Wood. I go past Bleaberry Tarn and climb upwards towards ___Ennerdale___ Forest. Here, I turn left and follow the long footpath south-east alongside the stream until I get to a building with a pirate name, called ___Black___ ___Sail___ ___Hut___ at 6-figure grid reference ___196124___ .

geog.1

pages 76-77

● **This is your chance to consider if glaciers really matter.**

1 Pages 76 and 77 in the student book tell us about five facts about glaciers. look at the list below and put them in rank order of importance, with 1 being the most important.

Facts about glaciers	Rank order
Glaciers bring in tourists.	
Glaciers present a challenge.	
Glaciers support life.	
Glaciers are in need of protection.	
Glaciers warn us about climate change.	

Pupils will make their own decisions about the relative importance of each of the facts.

2 Write three sentences explaining why you have chosen your number 1. Remember to give reasons for choosing it!

Three justifications for choosing their most significant fact, e.g. 'Glaciers are in need of protection':
Glaciers are in need of protection because they are beautiful.
Glaciers should be protected because many people visit them.
Glaciers should be protected because if global warming continues they may all be lost.

3 Design a poster in the space below showing what you know about glaciers. Use all the information that you have learned in this unit to help you.

Posters should include:
– when the British Isles was in the grip of ice
– facts about the world's glaciers today
– understanding of how glaciers shape the landscape
– landforms created by erosion and deposition
– how glacial landforms are shown on an OS map.

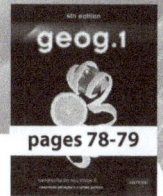

geog.1

pages 78-79

1

A 1	T 2	I 1	D 1	S 3	R 2	C 3	N 2

L 2	E 1	V 5	U 3	F 3	O 1	W 4	P 6

Look at the letter squares above. Each letter has a value. Use the letters to make as many words that you can that are to do with rivers. You can use each letter more than once. Which of your words is worth the most? What is the longest word you can make? Challenge others in your class!

Tip: Use page 79 in the student book to help you.

Possible answers are:

flood 8; water 10; river 11; source 13; attrition 14; runoff 14;

waterfall 18; floodplain 20; confluence 21; suspension 25

2 In the space below, write a paragraph about rivers. You must use all of the words that you found in your answer to the question above.

_____

_____

_____

_____

_____

_____

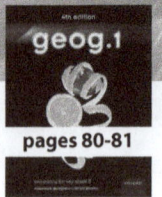

⬤ **This is where you will learn more about changes along England's longest river.**

1 The River Thames starts its life at Thames Head in the Cotswolds. Research what the river is like as it flows through each of the other places shown on the map below. Complete the table with the information you find. Show how the river looks different in the three places.

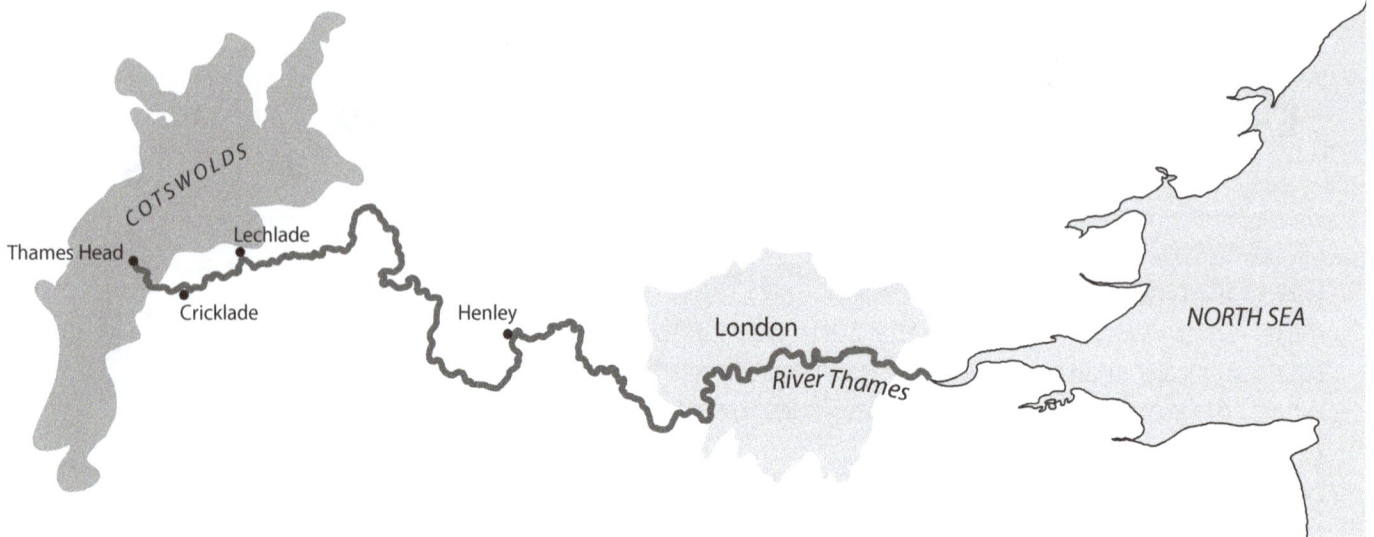

COTSWOLDS

Thames Head

Lechlade

Cricklade

Henley

London

River Thames

NORTH SEA

When the River Thames flows through ...	... it is like this:
Cricklade	Just a stream, wandering through meadows. Narrow; not big enough for boats, only canoes.
Lechlade	Quite wide. Deep enough for boats and barges.
Henley	Very wide. Large bridge and lots of boats.

This is about the water cycle, and how rainfall reaches a river.

1   Water moves between the ocean, the air and the land. This circulation is called the water cycle.

   a   Fill in the gaps below, choosing words from the box (you don't have to use them all).

   [2] The air _rises_. High up, where it's cooler, the water vapour _condenses_ into tiny water droplets. These form _clouds_.

   [4] The water drops fall as rain (or hail or sleet or snow).

   [1] The sun warms oceans, lakes and seas, turning water into water vapour. This is called _evaporation_.

   [5] Some water runs along the ground, and some soaks through it, heading for streams and rivers.

   [3] The droplets inside the clouds grow into larger droplets, leading to _precipitation_.

   [6] The river carries the water back to the _ocean_. The _cycle_ is complete. And then it starts all over again…

evaporation	rises	infiltration
gas	precipitation	clouds
condenses	ocean	cycle

   b   Add numbers in the small boxes so that the sentences are in the correct order.

2   Draw a diagram in the box below to show how rainwater reaches a river. Try to use as many of these words as possible (there are a few clues to help you!):

   interception (when rainwater catches leaves)   groundwater flow
   surface runoff   infiltration (the soaking of rainwater into the ground)
   throughflow   permeable (lets water soak through)
   groundwater   impermeable

   Students will refer to the diagram at the top of page 83 of the student book.

This is about the different parts of a river.

1 **a** Cross out the incorrect word in these sentences.

● The point where two rivers join is called a ~~tributary~~/confluence.
● The ~~confluence~~/watershed is an imaginary line that separates one drainage basin from the next.
● The ~~source~~/mouth is where the river flows into a lake, or the sea, or the ocean.
● The flat land around a river that gets flooded when the river overflows is the flood plain/~~tributary~~.
● The ~~mouth~~/source is the starting point of the river.
● The land around a river from which water drains into the river is the river basin/~~watershed~~.

b Now draw a sketch map of an imaginary river. Try to mark on and label all the features from **1a**.

Students will refer to the diagram on page 84 of the student book.

2 Fill in the gaps.

A drawing of the river's _long_ _profile_

The _source_ is the highest point.

The slope gets less steep in this middle stretch.

The _mouth_ is the river's lowest point.

lake or sea

different layers of rock below the river

Now the slope is flattening out.

5.4 A river at work

pages 86-87

This is about how rivers shape the land, by picking up, carrying and dropping material.

1   Fill in the gaps choosing words from the box.

Rivers do their work in three stages:

1 They pick up or _erode_ material from one place.

2 They carry or _transport_ it to another place

3 Then they drop or _deposit_ it.

| erode | transport | deposit |

2   Finish off this cartoon to tell the story of Sid the Stone's journey. (You don't have to fill all the boxes.)

Students will refer to the three diagrams on page 86 of the student book. As Sid is a small stone there is a good chance he will end up on the beach!

1

Sid the stone had lived in the river bank for as long as he could remember. Then, one day …

2

… he was prised out of the bank by **hydraulic action!**

3

4

5

6

Five landforms created by the river

This is about the landforms a river creates, by eroding and depositing material.

1 Fill in the gaps in this table.

Landform	Description	Created by ...
V-shaped valley	a valley shaped like the letter V, carved out by a river	erosion
waterfall	where the river water tumbles over a ledge of a hard rock	erosion
gorge	a narrow valley with steep sides	erosion
meander	a bend in a river	erosion + deposition
oxbow lake	a lake formed when a loop of river gets cut away	deposition

2 a These pictures show how a waterfall develops. Under each picture, describe what is going on.

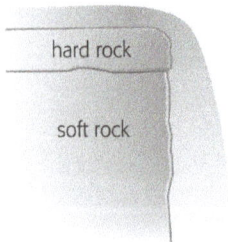

hard rock

soft rock

ledge undercut   plunge pool

waterfall retreats upstream

1 The river tumbles over a ledge of hard rock creating a waterfall.

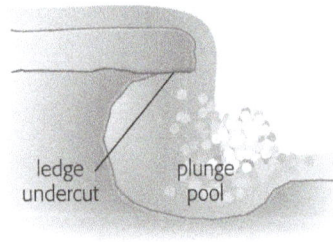

2 The soft rock below the ledge erodes, forming a plunge pool.

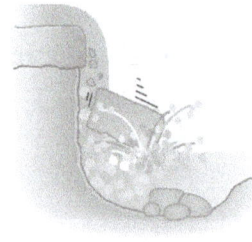

3 Eventually the ledge collapses into the plunge pool.

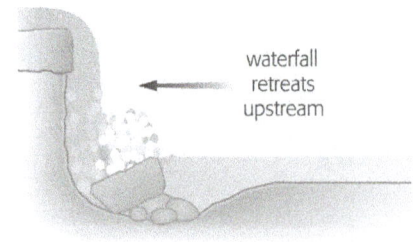

4 The process continues so that the waterfall gradually moves upstream.

b Draw pictures in the boxes below to show how a meander develops.

Students will refer to the diagrams at the top of page 89 of the student book.

Rivers and us

This is about how we make use of rivers and how sometimes we may damage them.

1 a Look at the statements below. Draw a line linking the statements that you think are connected. One has been done for you.

A Dams are built across some rivers — and then pumped to our taps

B Farmers pump water from rivers — and then sent back to rivers

C Water from rivers is cleaned — to irrigate their land

D Dirty water from our houses is cleaned — so that the water turns turbines to make electricity

b Choose one of your completed statements from A to D. Copy it out on the line below.

_____

c Do you think what you have just written is good or bad for the river? Give reasons for your answer.

The question asks clearly whether any of the statements is good or bad for the river (not for people). So some students may argue that dams and irrigation are bad for the river in that they remove water from it.

2 Read the speech bubbles below.

Rivers are for wildlife more than for people

Environmentalist

My fishing lines get caught by the boats and break

Fisherman

Without the water from the river my crops will not have enough water

Farmer

We are quiet and do not disturb anybody

Boat owner

There are very few places left where we can walk our dogs in peace

Dog walker

Choose the one person that you think may damage the river the most. Give reasons to explain your choice.

Answers will vary. The farmer may come out on top. Some students may point out that boat owners and walkers can damage the river banks.

Rivers **47**

This is where you will find out how rivers help keep you alive!

1 Cross out the incorrect word in these sentences.

   •   Across the UK water is pumped from rivers into ~~lakes~~ / reservoirs.

   •   A layer of rock that holds groundwater is called an ~~aquaplane~~ / aquifer.

   •   In a water treatment plant, chlorine is added to kill ~~fish~~ / germs.

   •   The clean water is then put in a storage reservoir and then from there it
       flows to ~~rivers~~ / homes.

   •   In a sewage plant the dirty water is cleaned up by bacteria / ~~oxygen~~.

   •   Clean water is put into ~~pipes~~ / rivers.

2 Carry out a survey about how, and where, water is used in your school.
   Write down five of your findings in the space below.

   Use the results to create an advert for your school website encouraging
   either adults *or* children to save water.

   | Tip: Remember who your target audience is, and be as persuasive as you can. | ! |

   Answers will vary but should include water for: sports fields; toilets; washing (in canteens or in wash rooms); cleaning the school; fire prevention.

How is water used in school?	Where is it used?
1	
2	
3	
4	
5	

Floods!

This is where you will find out how and why rivers flood.

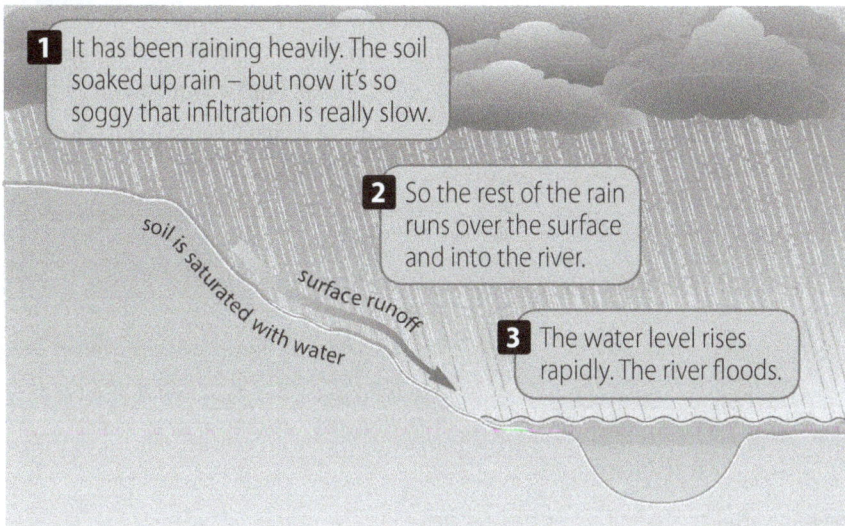

geog.1

pages 94-95

1. It has been raining heavily. The soil soaked up rain – but now it's so soggy that infiltration is really slow.

2. So the rest of the rain runs over the surface and into the river.

3. The water level rises rapidly. The river floods.

soil is saturated with water

surface runoff

1 a Look at the diagram above. In your own words explain what is meant by the following words and phrases.

Students should be given credit for rephrasing the explanations in the diagram.

Infiltration _____

_____

_____

_____

Surface runoff _____

_____

_____

_____

2 When floods happen people often talk about three things: flood prevention, flood defence and flood warning. In the spaces below write down what you think is meant by each term.

Flood prevention: *Taking measures to stop a flood taking place.*

Flood defence: *Taking measures to lessen the impact of a flood.*

Flood warning: *Letting people know when a flood is imminent so they can take precautions.*

3 Which of the three do you think is the most important? Give reasons why.

I think _____ is the most important because _____

Flood prevention is likely to be regarded as the most important.

Flooding on the River Thames

geog.1

pages 96-97

This is where you will think about the impacts of flooding on the River Thames.

1 Look at the photographs on page 96 in the student book that show flooding in Oxford, Abingdon and Twickenham. Imagine that was your house...and your local shop!

Describe, in the space below, how you and your family would cope with the floods.

Tip: Think about how it would change your daily life.

!

Students may have picked up information from news reports during the floods of 2013 (or more recent floods). Sandbags and moving precious items upstairs are two common measures. They may come up with more imaginative ideas.

2 Write down five things that you think it would be essential to save if your house got flooded. Explain your answers. *Answers will vary.*

I would save ...	because ...
1	
2	
3	
4	
5	

3 a Look at the statements below that show what people living by the River Thames may do if their area became flooded. Put them in priority order, by writing the numbers 1-5 by each. Number 1 would be the first thing that you think they should do, and 5 the last.

Answers will vary. Students need to be aware that turning off the power is a major priority.

Ring family		Phone 999		Turn off power		Save pets		Move upstairs	

b In the space below give reasons to explain your first choice.

My first choice is _____

This is because _____

_____

_____

This is where you will think about the impacts of flooding on the River Thames.

1 Read this information about London. Do you think London should be protected by another Thames Barrier? Fill in the speech bubbles below to show your thoughts.

The information will leave students with a strong impression that a second barrier would be a good idea. There is the suggestion of a 'soft' solution – the emergency flood plain – and their attention may need to be drawn to this. How effective (including cost-effective) this alternative is likely to be is not mentioned.

- London's population is 8.17 million (2011 data) and growing

- Architect Sir Terry Farrell has proposed building a five-mile barrage from Southend to Sheerness - basically the mouth of the Thames - all linked by islands.

- A second barrier could house turbines and use tide flows to generate electricity for London.

- The Farrell proposal includes a road and rail bridge to create a transport link between the two counties and the islands could be used for housing and leisure facilities, the sale of which will help pay for it all.

- Another idea is to set aside large areas of open country downstream of London as emergency flood plains, so protecting the London.

- London's exports add up to about 24 per cent of the total value of all UK exports

- The Thames Barrier took eight years to build, costing £535m (£1600m at 2013 prices) and became fully working in 1982.

- Europe's largest shopping centre is in London - Westfield in Stratford, near the Olympic Park

- "The Thames Barrier was built in response to the floods in 1953. Nobody had heard of global warming then." Dr Richard Bloore (January 2013)

- In 2007 a second Thames barrier was costed at £20 billion.

- The Thames Barrier was originally designed to work until the year 2030.

- There are 270 stations on London's underground tube network

- 3.4 million visitors came to London in the first three months of 2013

- The average house price in London (May 2013) is £437,000

- Climate change is causing sea level rise, which could mean larger storm surges in the Thames.

- The Thames Barrier currently protects 125sq km of London, including an estimated 1.25m people, £80bn worth of property, a large proportion of the London tube network and many historic buildings, power supplies, hospitals and schools.

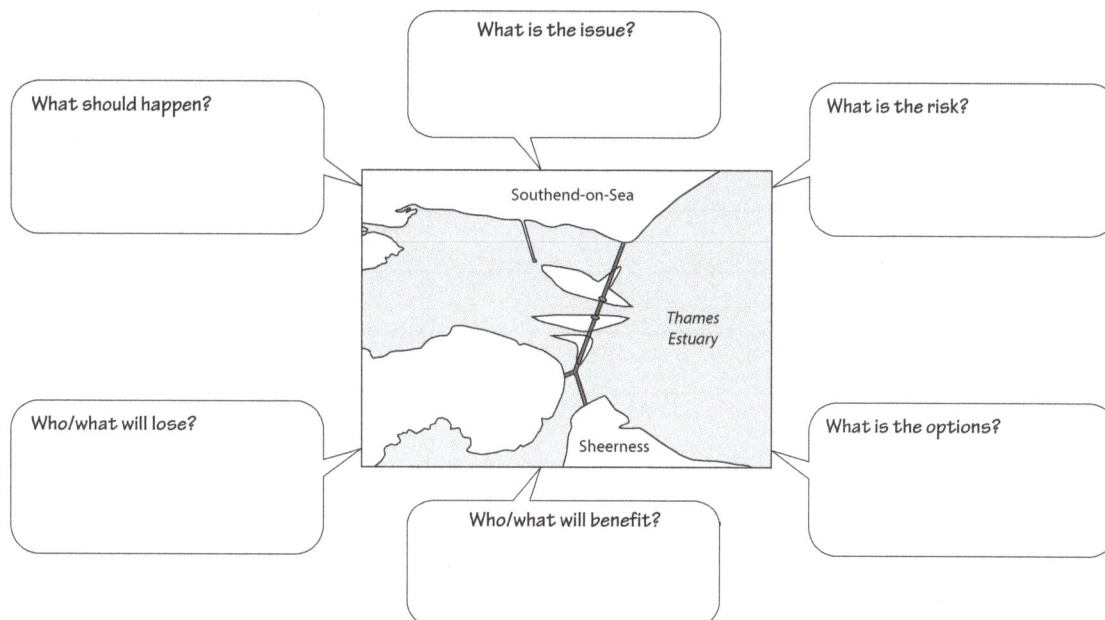

What is the issue?

What should happen?

What is the risk?

Southend-on-Sea

Thames Estuary

Who/what will lose?

What is the options?

Sheerness

Who/what will benefit?

geog.1

pages 100-101

This test relies on the students not looking up a map of Africa, including the maps in this chapter.

1 Test yourself. Without looking anywhere else, draw an outline of Africa in the box on the left. Then draw in the borders of all the countries you can think of. Include the names of cities, mountains, rivers, lakes and deserts.

2 Write down all you know about three of the places you have put on the map.

Place 1 _____

_____

Place 2 _____

_____

Place 3 _____

_____

3 At the end of this topic, come back and see if you've been correct about these places. Draw a ☺ next to each place you got more or less right. If you were wrong draw a ☹ next to the place!

geog.1
pages 102-103

This is about locating the continent of Africa on the world map.

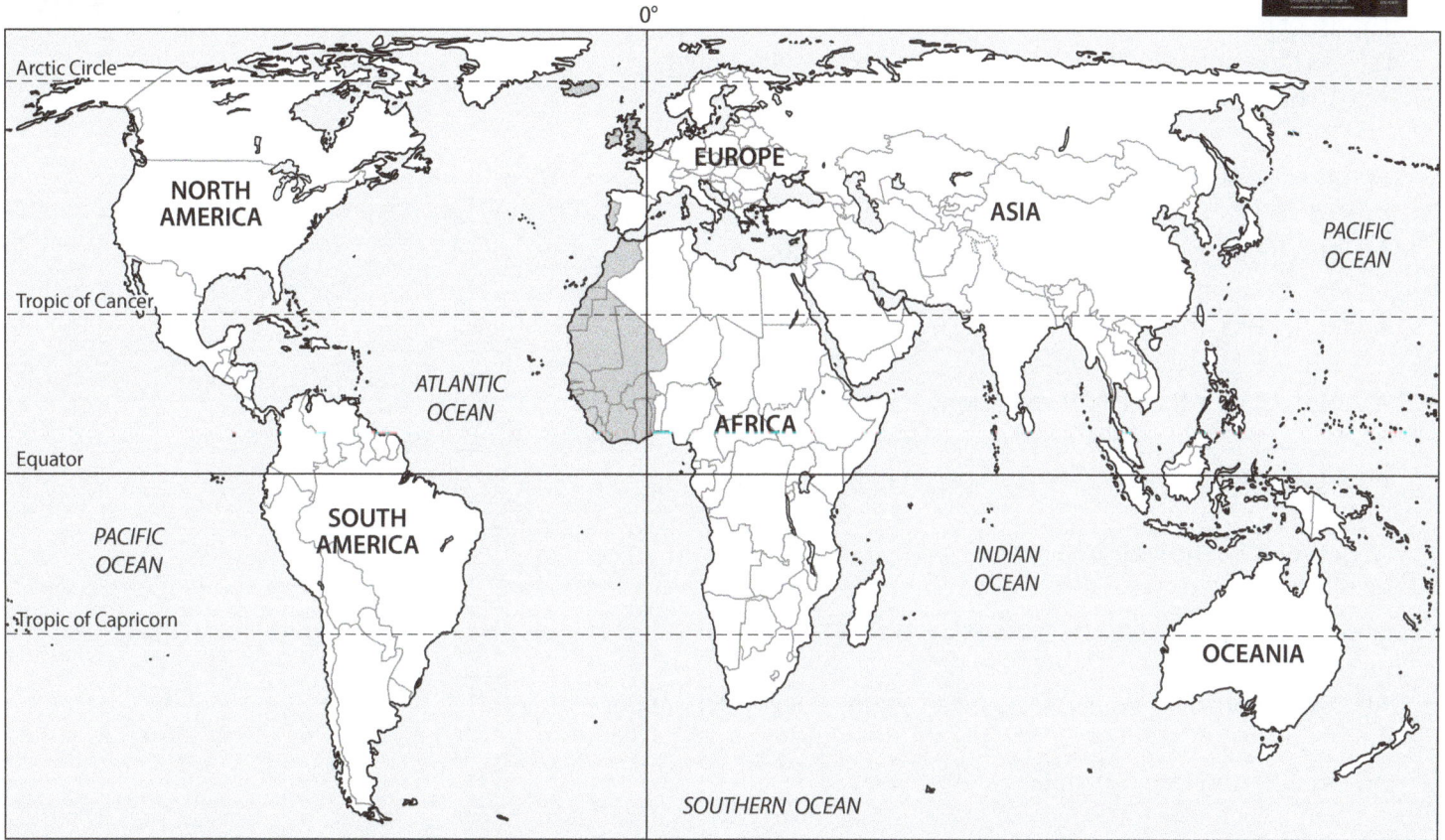

1 Colour in all the land in the world that lies between the Tropic of Cancer and the Tropic of Capricorn. This area is known as the 'tropics' and is the hottest part of the world.

a Which continent has most of its land area inside the tropics? _Africa_

b Which continent lies completely outside the tropics? _Europe_

2 Using a second colour fill in all the land area of Africa that lies outside the tropics. What proportion of Africa lies outside the tropics? Circle the correct answer.

A About 60%   B About 75%   C About 35%

3 The map also shows 0° longitude, which is known as the Prime Meridian. It runs through Greenwich in London. The countries that share the Greenwich Meridian Time Zone (GMT) with the UK have been shaded on the map.

a How many of the countries in Africa which share the same time zone as us can you name?

Students may refer to the political map of Africa on page 108 of the student book (or this information).

_____

_____

This is an exercise in placing key events in African history into the correct order.

1 The list of ten key events in African history below has been jumbled up. Put the list into the right order in which the events occurred by writing a number from 1 to 10 in each box.

About AD 1400. The Kingdom of Kongo begins. `6`

About 60 000 years ago. Homo Sapiens leaves Africa. `3`

About AD 1800. The Atlantic Slave Trade is ended. `8`

AD 1951. Libya is the first African colony to gain independence. `9`

About 2 million years ago. The first species of human appears. `1`

About AD 800. The Mali Empire begins. `5`

About 200 000 years ago. Homo Sapiens appears. `2`

AD 1980. Zimbabwe, Britain's last African colony, gains independence `10`

AD 1420. Portuguese exploration of Africa begins. `7`

About 3000 BC. The Ancient Egyptian civilization begins. `4`

2 Two African countries, shaded on the map below, were never European colonies. Name these two countries and write about them below.

Country A _Liberia_
Answers will vary, but look for an account of its
origins as a home for freed American slaves.
_____

Country B _Ethiopia_
Answers will vary but should include its
successful war against the Italian colonizers.
_____

6.3 Africa today

This is about looking at population growth figures and asking questions about them.

 geog.1

pages 106-107

The population of Africa is expected to double in the next 35 years.
But the figures for the whole of Africa do not tell the full story.

1 The table below shows the population figures (in millions) for six of the largest
African countries for 1950 and 2013 and the projected figures up to 2100.

	1950	2013	2025	2050	2100
Democratic Republic of Congo	12	68	92	155	262
Egypt	22	82	97	122	135
Ethiopia	18	94	125	188	243
Nigeria	38	174	240	440	913
South Africa	14	53	57	63	64
Tanzania	8	49	69	129	275

* UN figures

a Which country grew, or is projected to grow the fastest between;

1950-2013 _Tanzania_ ? 2013-2100 _Tanzania_ ?

b Which country grew or is projected to grow the slowest between;

1950-2013 _Egypt_ ? 2013-2100 _South Africa_ ?

c Which country is projected to grow faster between 2013-2100 than it has
grown between 1950-2013? _Nigeria_

2 a These figures are a 'medium variant' estimate; they could go up or down. What
factors could cause these figures to vary? _Factors should include:_

disease, birth control, womens education, immigration (refugees).

b The projected figures for South Africa show a very small increase in population.
Can you give an explanation for this? _Better education and improved living standards._

c What needs to happen for the projected figures of the other countries to show a
similar decline in growth? _As above._

3 Use this map to work out the official languages of the
following countries:

A Angola _Portugese_   B Chad _French_

C Equatorial Guinea _Spanish_   D Gabon _French_

E Ghana _English_   F Uganda _English_

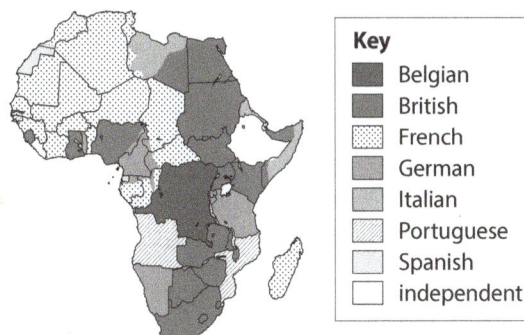

Key	
■	Belgian
■	British
▦	French
■	German
■	Italian
▨	Portuguese
□	Spanish
□	independent

Africa **55**

This will help you understand Africa's size and the variety of its countries.

Country	
Algeria	1
Angola	7
Benin	38
Botswana	22
Burkina Faso	29
Burundi	44
Cameroon	24
Cape Verde	50
Central African Republic	20
Chad	5
Comoros	51
Côte d'Ivoire	28
Dem. Rep. Congo	2
Djibouti	47
Egypt	12
Equatorial Guinea	45
Eritrea	36
Ethiopia	10
Gabon	30
Gambia	49
Ghana	32
Guinea	31
Guinea-Bissau	42
Kenya	23
Lesotho	43
Liberia	39
Libya	4
Madagascar	21
Malawi	37
Mali	8
Mauritania	11
Mauritius	52
Morocco	25
Mozambique	16
Namibia	15
Niger	6
Nigeria	14
Republic of Congo	27
Rwanda	46
São Tomé and Príncipe	53
Senegal	34
Seychelles	54
Sierra Leone	40
Somalia	19
South Africa	9
South Sudan	18
Sudan	3
Swaziland	48
Tanzania	13
Togo	41
Tunisia	35
Uganda	33
Zambia	17
Zimbabwe	26

1 Using the scale on the map above find out how far it is between the following African capital cities.

   a Algiers and Pretoria _7500 km_   b Cairo and Abuja _3400 km_

   c Addis Ababa and Bamako _5100 km_   d Mogadishu and Banjul _7000 km_

2 Compare distances in the British Isles with distances in Africa. Name two African capital cities that are about the same distance apart as:

   a London and Cardiff _e.g. Accra and Lome_

   b Belfast and Cardiff _e.g. Gaborone and Pretoria_

   c London and Edinburgh _e.g. Kampala and Bujumbura_ .

   d Into which African country would the island of Britain fit easily both north-south and east-west? _Algeria is the best fit. Democratic Republic of Congo and Sudan would be lighter._

3 Can you guess the size of Africa's countries? Just looking at the map and using a ruler try to guess what the order of size is of Africa's 54 countries. Write in numbers from 1 (largest) to 54 (smallest) in the boxes alongside the names of the countries. Compare your guesses with a partner's, then look up the answers to see who was the closest!

Population distribution in Africa

This looks at population differences between African regions and selected countries.

More and more Africans are moving from the countryside to towns or big cities. Here are the rural and urban population percentages for the different African regions.

Region	Urban	Rural
Eastern	23.6%	76.4%
Central	43.1%	56.9%
Northern	51.2%	48.8%
Southern	58.7%	41.3%
Western	44.9%	55.1%

1   Complete the pie graphs below to show the rural and urban divisions within the African regions. One has been done for you.

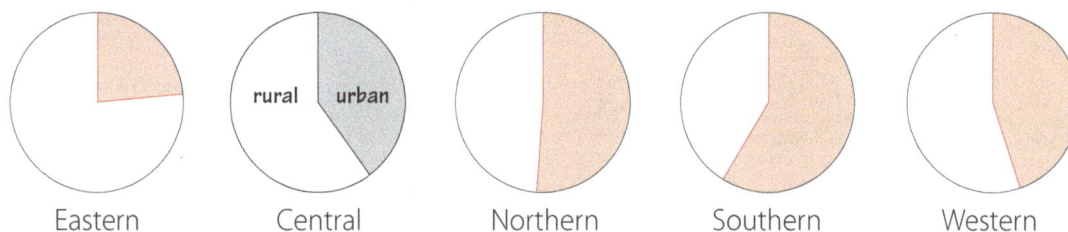

rural | urban

Eastern   Central   Northern   Southern   Western

Look back at the table in 6.3 showing population projections for six African countries. They represent all of the African regions.

2   Write down which regions they are in: Tanzania and Ethiopia _Eastern_   Egypt _Northern_

Nigeria _Western_   South Africa _Southern_   Democratic Republic of Congo _Central_

3   The six countries in the table have the largest populations in their regions. So their urban/rural differences reflect the regions they are in. What links might there be between rural/urban differences and their rate of population increase?

The better education that urban dwellers have access to is likely to mean a decrease in population increase over time as girls become better educated. Poorer health care in the rural areas may offset this difference but in some countries health care is reaching the rural areas more than it once did. So you would expect the Eastern region to have the highest rate of population increase.

Here are the percentages of the populations of the six countries that are under 14 (your generation!)

DRC = 45%   Egypt = 31.1%   Ethiopia = 42.7%   Nigeria = 44.4%   South Africa = 29.5%   Tanzania = 44.9%

4   How might the proportion of the population that is under the age of 14 be connected to their rate of population increase?

The larger the proportion of the young population the greater the population increase as that 'bulge' reaches the age of fertility. So the population of Tanzania is bound to increase rapidly for a while however successful current attempts are to limit population growth.

5   Can you name any other factors that might be used in predicting the future population of a country?

Looking at other developing countries that are further down the road of increased urbanisation and industrial development to see what happened to their population growths. Generally speaking, families begin to limit their size as their material aspirations and their ambitions for their children increase.

6.6 **Africa: physical features**

Here we look at the relationship between Africa's physical features
and its countries.

geog.1
pages 112-113

1 Compare this map with the political map on
page 56 and answer the following questions;

a Which countries are the Atlas Mountains in?

   Morocco and Algeria

b In which countries is the Kalahari Desert?

   Botswana and Namibia

c In which country is Mount Kilimanjaro?

   Tanzania

d In which country are the Tibesti Mountains?

   Chad

e In which country does the River Benue rise?

   Cameroon

2 On the map circle those places where rivers form the borders or part of the
borders between African countries. Name these rivers and the countries either
side of them. [Note that rivers sometimes form a part but not all of the border
between countries.]

3 What is unusual about the River Cubango?

   It discharges into an island delta, the Okavango swamp instead of the sea.

4 Research and find out what is unusual about Lake Volta.

   It is a man-made reservoir, the largest in the world.

This is about telling what biome a place is in from its weather statistics.

The letters on the map represent five cities:

Dodoma   Tamanrasset   Yaoundé   Gaborone   Addis Ababa

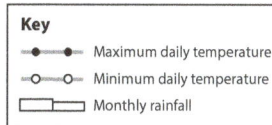

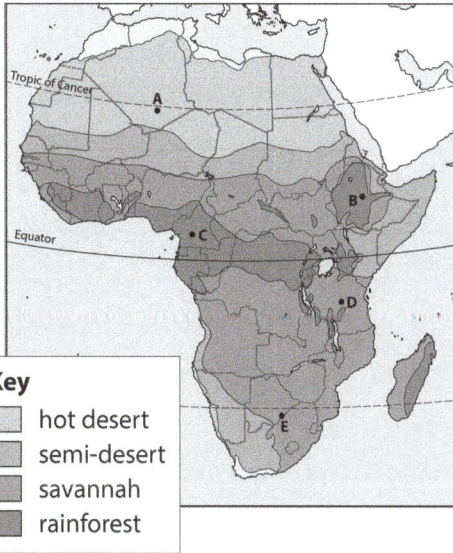

Key
- Maximum daily temperature
- Minimum daily temperature
- Monthly rainfall

Here are the climate charts for these places. Match each place on the map to a numbered chart and write down which biome it represents (hot desert, semi-desert, savanna, rainforest and mountain) Bear in mind the height above sea level (elevation) of each place when looking at the temperature figures. Also write down the reasons you matched that place to its biome.

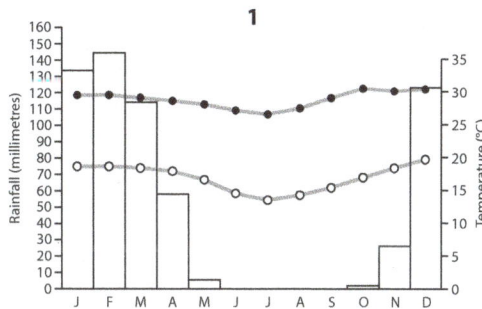

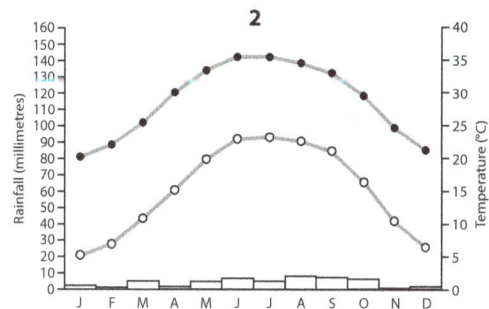

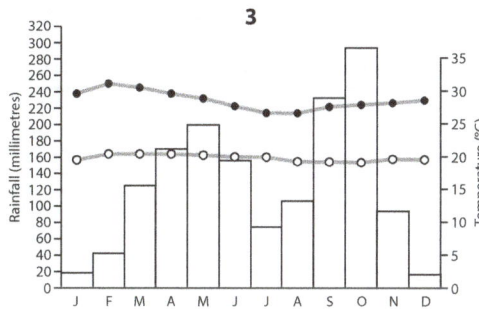

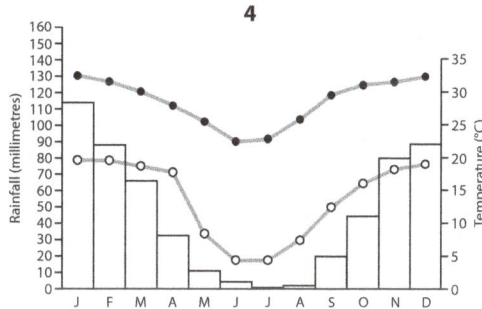

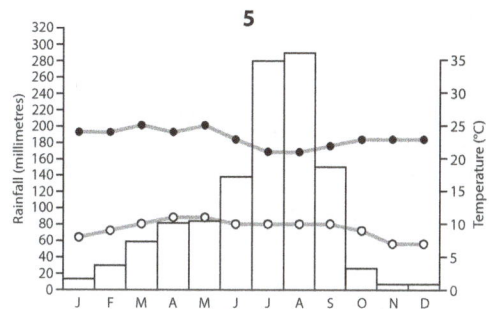

Key
- hot desert
- semi-desert
- savannah
- rainforest

Place A (elevation 1320 m)   Chart number _2_   Name _Tamanrasset_   Biome _Desert_

Reasons _Very low rainfall and considerable variation between maximum and minimum daily temperatures._

Place B (elevation 2355 m)   Chart number _5_   Name _Addis Ababa_   Biome _Mountain_

Reasons _Although near the equator, the temperatures are reduced due to elevation. Also big variation between day and night temperatures._

Place C (elevation 726 m)   Chart number _3_   Name _Yaoundé_   Biome _Rainforest_

Reasons _High temperature throughout the year with high rainfall._

Place D (elevation 1120 m)   Chart number _1_   Name _Dodoma_   Biome _Savannah_

Reasons _High temperatures but pronounced seasonal rainfall._

Place E (elevation 983 m)   Chart number _4_   Name _Gaborone_   Biome _Savannah_

Reasons _Like Dodoma but closer to semi-desert. Greater variation in daily temperatures. Lower rainfall._

1 The Horn of Africa is a region of north-east Africa. Use an atlas to find out the closest non-African country to the Horn.

  a What is the name of this country? _Yemen_

  b Which country in the Horn is this country closest to? _Djibouti_

  c Approximately how far apart are the two countries? _Approximately 20 km_

2 Use the student book and your own research to complete the following sentences. Cross out the wrong word from each pair.

The Horn of Africa is a ~~country~~ / region in the north east / ~~north west~~ of Africa. In total, ~~five~~ / four countries make up the region. Much of the coastline is along the ~~Pacific~~ / Indian Ocean which forms the coast of ~~Ethiopia~~ / Somalia. Many of the people who live in the Horn are ~~tourists~~ / nomads whose main work is farming / ~~mining~~. ~~Djibouti~~ / Addis Ababa is the largest city in Ethiopia with a population of 4.2 / 6.8 million people.

3 Use the globe below to help you describe the location of the Horn of Africa. Write your answers around the globe.

> Tip: Remember to use as many geographical words as you can. **!**

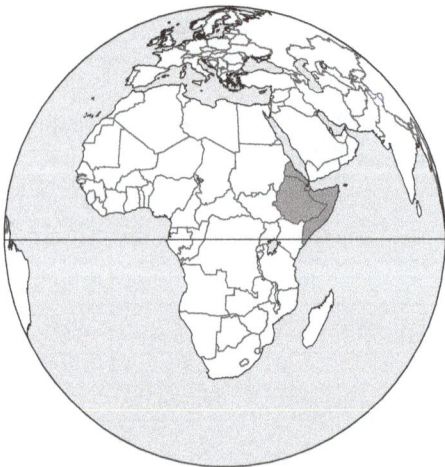

Responses should refer only to the location of the Horn. A typical answer might read:
The Horn of Africa is in East Africa and lies just north of the Equator. It is bordered by Kenya, Sudan and South Sudan to the south and west, and the Indian Ocean, the Gulf of Aden and the Red Sea to the north.

4 How would you get to the Horn of Africa from Southampton in the UK if you were travelling by sea? Use an atlas to plan a route. Describe where your ship would sail.

> Tip: Remember to use geographical words and the names of countries in your answer! **!**

Two possible routes can be explored here. South into the Atlantic, down the west coast of Africa and then into the Indian Ocean at the Cape of Good Hope, then north along the east African coast. Alternatively, into the Mediterranean Sea and then the Suez Canal into the Red Sea.

Now you will find out more about the lives of people who live in the Horn of Africa.

1 Many of the people who live in the Horn live in straw and mud huts, as shown in the photograph on page 119 in the student book. Here is a description of the huts...

The people in this part of Eritrea are pastoral farmers, and keep animals. The people live in round huts made from an interweaving of rods and twigs covered with clay. The thatched, cone-shaped roofs go right down to the ground, making the hut look a little like a 'beehive'. Inside there are mats, often made of woven goat hair. The huts often have two entrances and are usually found in clusters away from main tracks, surrounded by low fences. It is often quite a walk to find water.

In the space below make a drawing of what you think the huts will look like. Use the description to help you. Remember to add some labels.

The drawing, with labels, should reflect the descriptive text above. Key features of the huts are likely to be that they are round, thatched and beehive-like. The huts have two entrances and are clustered together, surrounded by low fences.

2 Imagine you live in one of these huts with your family. Write a description of what a typical day might be like. Particularly focus on the adjectives that you use and underline the three best adjectives in your answer. Compare your answer with a partner.

A variety of answers are possible, depending upon what the pupils feel are significant features of the peoples' lives. Descriptive adjectives, however, should be used with the best three underlined.

geog.1

pages 120-121

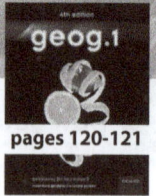

This is where you will get physical with this part of Africa!

1 The main physical features of the Horn are listed below. Rank them 1-4, with 1 being your first choice. Which area of the Horn that you would most like to visit? Give two reasons for your answer.

Ethiopian Highlands ☐   Afar Triangle ☐   Ogaden ☐   Coast ☐

Pupil answers will depend upon their own views about the regions. Answers should relate two reasons for visiting the chosen region.

2 Write a fifty word radio advert that would 'sell' your choice to tourists and visitors. Remember your use of adjectives and geographical vocabulary. And it must be *exactly* 50 words!

Exactly fifty words that offer a persuasive argument for visiting the chosen region. As it is a radio advert, language used should be carefully chosen to be very expressive.

3 Research your chosen area and create a fact file. Write your answers in the boxes below.

Six relevant and interesting facts about the chosen region.

Fact 1:

Fact 6:

Fact 2:

My area is

_____

Fact 5:

Fact 4:

Fact 3:

This is about climate and how it affects farmers and their families.

1 Look at the climate facts below. Next to each, write one effect that each would have on farmers. *Suggested answers below.*

Climate fact	Effect
The lower land is hot all year.	As a result crops need a lot of water.
Rain does not fall steadily through the year.	Farmers have to try to store water: very difficult in such a hot climate.
Some areas have two dry seasons each year.	Keeping water for irrigation is difficult.
In many areas July temperatures exceed 30°C.	Crops can shrivel and die. Hard to work in the heat.
During some years the rains fail completely	This can cause famine and people die.

2 You have been asked to write a summary of the climate in the Horn of Africa for a geography website. Use maps A and B on page 122, and the map on page 118, in the student book to help you.

Tip: Remember to use geographical terms, compass directions and also country names in your answer!

A typical answer may be:

The Horn of Africa is generally hot all year, although in the mountains to the west it is cooler. Some places have very little rainfall, particularly large parts of Somalia. There are both rainy and dry seasons. In the drier areas near the coast, the rains are not reliable.

3 Imagine you are a farmer in the Horn of Africa. Describe where you think it would be best to farm and give reasons for your answer. Write your answer in the speech bubble below.

Pupils may choose to grow crops, coffee or rear animals. Their choice will determine where they choose to farm, but should be accompanied by more than one reason.
Crops: the higher lands of Ethiopia and Eritrea where there is more rainfall and July temperatures are cooler.
Coffee: mainly in Ethiopia, on the higher land where there is more rainfall and slightly lower temperatures.
Animals: farmers can rear animals across the region as the nomads travel with their animals to find food for them. Animals do not need as much water as crops and can travel to find it.

This is about how Ethiopian coffee farmers try to cope with the challenges they face.

Oromia Coffee Farmers' Co-operative Union was founded in 1999. Its members are local farmers in southern and south west Ethiopia which produces two-thirds of the country's coffee. The farms are located in mountainous, rainforest areas at altitudes of 1,500 to 2,000 metres where electricity and clean running water are rare. The co-operative exports and sells coffee on behalf of the farmers and some of the profits are then used to support social projects such as schools and health care. It aims to help its members to become economically self-sufficient and make sure that families can feed themselves if harvests fail, which could lead to famine. It also aims to help farmers cope better with changes in world coffee prices that can affect their income.

Coffee is a globally traded commodity just like oil. Prices go up and down because of factors such as changing weather conditions in the major producing countries, political unrest, worries about now much may be grown (too much or too little), changing transport costs (which is influenced by the number one commodity, oil!) and other unexpected factors. These may include news of a possible drought or freezing conditions in coffee producing areas which would likely mean that there is less coffee available globally. Prices would then go up.

Coffee "C" Futures US cents/pound

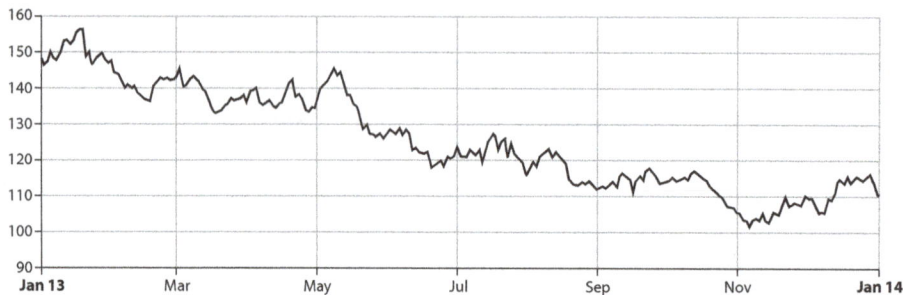

1 Read the information above and study the graph of world coffee prices. Write down one farming challenge, and one economic challenge, that Ethiopian coffee farmers face.

Farming challenge: Coffee is grown in mountainous areas where clean running water and electricity is not always available.

Economic challenge: Coffee prices change a lot, so it is difficult for the farmers to know how much they will earn from their crop.

2 Write a description of what happened to world coffee prices during 2013. What problems would these bring to both coffee farmers and the Oromia Cooperative?

Coffee prices have generally fallen in 2013. This means the farmers would earn less money which will affect themselves and their families. They may not be able to buy enough food. The co-operative will suffer because the less money that is earned through coffee sales will mean that less can be spent on schools and health care.

3 Find out how much of your own family's shopping is Fair Trade. Are there things that you buy that are not, but could be? Make a family shopping list of Fair Trade items.

Answers will vary.

4 Look at where the items on your shopping list have come from. Mark the countries on a world map. What do you notice about where your items come from? Compare your answer with a partner; do you notice any patterns?

Answers will vary.

7.5 Life as a nomad

geog.1

pages 126-127

This is about the nomads, who live and travel with their animals.

1 Complete the following statements, using the words from the box.

grazing
portable
fertile
animals
seasonal
dry

- Nomads are people who rear _animals_ .

- Nomads live in the _dry_ areas of the Horn of Africa.

- Nomads travel with their animals to find _grazing_ .

- Rivers that flow in the rainy season are called _seasonal_ .

- Land that is not good to grow crops on is called not _fertile_ .

- The homes of many Nomad's move; the homes are _portable_ .

2 Look at the photograph below showing nomads at a well. Imagine you are there as an investigative journalist for a UK newspaper. You have been asked to write about the lives of the nomads.

Write a report of your visit: what are the people doing? Write down what you see, hear and smell.

Answers should relate to each of the three senses identified:
sight, hearing and smell. Expect good use of adjectives.

3 What do you think is the greatest challenge that nomads face in their daily lives? Write your answer below and give reasons for your choice.

This may relate to the harsh existence (always travelling),
lack of money earned or the difficulty in having to carry
food or indeed find food as they travel.

Working as a salt miner

This is about the future for the Danakil depression, one of the world's most hostile environments.

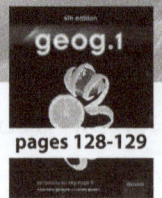

1   Dallol, a remote mining camp only accessible by camel, is found in the Danakil Depression. Read these facts and then tick the correct box next to them. Does the fact refer to the past, the present or the future?

Tip: You can tick more than one box!

	Past	Present	Future
It was once a busy site mining potash, sylvite, and salt.	✓		
In 1906, when the salt was discovered, an Italian mining company built a railway to the coast.	✓		
Getting to Dallol from any direction is long and difficult.	✓	✓	✓
The locals refer to the area as "the Gateway to Hell."		✓	
China and India have agreed to help Ethiopia build 5,000 km of railway giving access to the Danakil potash region.		✓	✓
Thin crust covers pools of acid, bubbling to the surface through hot springs and geysers which spit out toxic gases.	✓	✓	✓
Djibouti has close proximity to India, the second largest importer of potash.		✓	
There are currently no medical facilities in the region.		✓	
The harbour facilities in Djibouti are being upgraded.		✓	✓
At Dallol, salt deposits reach the earth's surface, which made mining more profitable.	✓		
Today the town has long been abandoned, only parts of the salt-block walls of buildings remain.		✓	

	Past	Present	Future
The journey by camel can take a full day from the nearest village.	✓	✓	✓
Allana Potash plans to spend $642m in three years on four projects in Ethiopia's northeast.			✓
A Canadian company, Allana Potash, was granted a mining permit on 9 October, 2013.	✓	✓	✓
There is the threat of "fire wind," the hot sandstorms which have been described as feeling like a 'tornado in an oven'.		✓	✓
In 2011, the global demand for fertilizer totalled 185 million tonnes, with over 50 million tonnes being potassium-based.	✓		
Two communities in the area are being resettled as a health and safety precaution in early 2014.	✓	✓	
Potash is a potassium-based mineral used in fertilizer.	✓	✓	✓
A new road will cross the Danakil basin, an important link for importing equipment and the export of the potash.			✓
A tourist accidently fell into a natural sulphur spring at Mount Dallol, a popular tourist attraction, suffering burns to 35% of the body.	✓		

2   What do you think the future holds for Dallol – should the company be allowed to mine?

If you were in charge of planning for the region's future, what decisions would you make? Why? What impact will your decision have, and on who?

Answers should cite decisions, reasons for them and the impacts of that decision.

7.7 Life on the coast

geog.1

pages 130-131

This is about the opportunities for tourism in the Horn of Africa.

1 The countries in the Horn of Africa have many physical (natural) advantages. Identify three of these advantages and say why they could be attractive to tourists.

Physical (natural) advantage	Attractive to tourists because...
Varied landscape	landscapes to suit different tourist tastes
Long coastline	beach holidays possible
Mountainous areas	good for hiking

2 Read the extract below.

Mo Farah was born in Mogadishu in Somalia in 1983. His double Olympic gold gives a much-needed positive image for Somalia whose name has unfortunately become linked with anarchy and lawlessness. In 2014 the UK and USA Governments both still advised against travelling to the country.

However, Somalia has many features that could prove attractive to tourists, not least its Indian Ocean white sandy beaches. Lido Beach, Mogadishu's most popular stretch of coast, offers visitors a beach scene that is common in much of Europe and beyond – ice cream, cold drinks, and children playing in the sea whilst young adults play football. There are street cafés and fruit sellers – all seemingly representing the 'typical' tourist destination. Tourism is one area of the economy that Somalia is very keen to develop.

Look at the list below showing some of the things people consider when deciding where to go on holiday. Circle each 'emoticon' to show the extent to which you think Somalia meets these expectations.

Tip: You may need to do some research as well as using the student book to help you!

Wide range of activities ☹ ☺ ☺
Ease of getting there ☹ ☺ ☺
Interesting history ☹ ☺ ☺
Good hotels ☹ ☺ ☺
Reputation of the tourist destination ☹ ☺ ☺
The weather ☹ ☺ ☺
The food ☹ ☺ ☺
Safety ☹ ☺ ☺

A wide variety of answers possible depending on research done.

3 What do you think Somalia should do to encourage more tourism? Prepare a five point plan that would help them.

Answers should consist of five points.

7.8 In the city: Addis Ababa

This is where you find out more about Ethiopia's capital city.

pages 132-133

1 Cross out the wrong word or phrase in each sentence.

- Addis Ababa is home to the ~~European Union~~ / African Union.
- You will see many fine buildings, shopping centres and ~~old~~ / modern blocks of flats.
- A lot of people are unemployed, over a quarter / ~~half~~ of the workforce.
- Many of the slums / ~~houses~~ in the city are rented out by the government at a very low rent.
- The population of Addis Ababa is growing fast / ~~slowly~~.

2 Here are some facts about Addis Ababa. Colour the one that you think proves most challenging for the city to deal with. Write three ways in which the city could cope with the issue.

A birth rate of 23 for every thousand people

The average life expectancy is around 65 years

The population will double about every 33 years

50% of the people live in poverty

Addis Ababa

20% of the population are under 15 years old

Its population of 4.2 million grows by 140 000 each year

39% of the population can read and write

Over 25% of the population have no job

A variety of answers are possible. Whichever is chosen should be supported by three ways in which the city could cope, e.g. '50% of people live in poverty': The city could offer free work-based training for all; the city could establish self-help schemes and food banks; the government could encourage more investment which will help to produce jobs.

3 You are lucky – you have been awarded a new flat in the lottery! Write an email to your family in the countryside explaining how you feel about the news.

This should be quite a happy email! Feelings about moving into a new flat should be clearly communicated.

Here you can learn about some of the difficult dilemmas that Djibouti faces.

geog.1
pages 134–135

May 2012: After six years of consecutive drought, Djibouti faces severe food insecurity. Food production from both crops and livestock remains extremely poor. Many rural households have migrated within their region or moved into the towns looking for work. Households unable to afford to move have suffered serious livestock loss and the amount of farmed land has dropped sharply. As more than 90 per cent of food is imported, the country is highly susceptible to global price changes. The poor, who spend up to three quarters of their income on food, are particularly vulnerable to high food prices. (Adapted from http://www.wfp.org/countries/djibouti)

August 2013: the United Nations High Commissioner for Refugees (UNHCR) reported that Djibouti had been receiving refugees and asylum seekers from neighbouring countries for many years. There have been steady arrivals of people fleeing their countries for a combination of reasons, such as war and civil unrest, persecution and poverty.

December 2013: Djibouti's Energy Minister signed an agreement with a Chinese transnational electricity company for the construction of a 90 km power line. The project will help supply energy to the planned 784 km railway line, announced in July 2013, which will link Djibouti to Addis Ababa in Ethiopia.

1   The Djibouti government have to make decisions about where to spend the limited amount of money that the country has. Complete the table below.

Issue	What is the issue?	Is it good or bad for Djibouti? Why?
Issue 1: May 2012 Food insecurity	Food may not always be available as they depend upon imports	Bad as they cannot always guarantee to have enough food to feed the people and it also may be too expensive for them to buy.
Issue 2: Aug 2013 Refugees	Many people are homeless and arrive in Djibouti from other countries	Bad as it puts an extra strain on the country's resources. However, it provides a workforce that the country could utilise and brings rich cultural differences to the country.
Issue 3: Dec 2013 Electricity line	Electricity will be accessible for more people	Good that electricity may be more freely available. Bad because the project is being managed by a foreign company which may be risky.

2   The government has to prioritise its spending. Where do you think it should spend its money? Who would benefit? Choose one of the issues above. Give reasons for your answer.

I think that issue 1 / 2 / 3 should be the government's priority because _____

A clear reason for the decision must be given.

This is where you will use data to help understand more about the Horn.

geog.1

pages 136-137

1 Imagine you live in one of the countries in the Horn of Africa. You have been asked to give your five greatest hopes for the region in the future – your own wish list of progress or changes that you would like to see happen. What would you put on your wish list and why? Use data from pages 136-137 to help support your answer.

Wish 1 The wishes should all be positive and each should be justified.

Wish 2

Wish 3

Wish 4

Wish 5

2 Now think about everything that you have learned about the Horn of Africa. Draw a picture that represents what you understand the Horn to be like. Use labels and try to be as creative as possible!

A creative and representative picture should be attempted.